D1592552

Andreas Vieth (Hrsg.)
Richard Rorty

8. Münstersche Vorlesungen zur Philosophie 2004
8th Münster Lectures on Philosophy 2004

mit / with

Richard Rorty

Andreas Vieth (Hrsg.)

Richard Rorty

His Philosophy Under Discussion

ontos
verlag

Frankfurt I Paris I Ebikon I Lancaster I New Brunswick

Bibliographic information published by Die Deutsche Bibliothek
Die Deutsche Bibliothek lists this publication in the Deutsche Nationalbibliographie;
detailed bibliographic data is available in the Internet at http://dnb.ddb.de

North and South America by
Transaction Books
Rutgers University
Piscataway, NJ 08854-8042
trans@transactionpub.com

United Kingdom, Ire Iceland, Turkey, Malta, Portugal by
Gazelle Books Services Limited
White Cross Mills
Hightown
LANCASTER, LA1 4XS
sales@gazellebooks.co.uk

©2005 ontos verlag
P. O. Box 15 41, D-63133 Heusenstamm nr. Frankfurt
Tel. ++(49) 6104 66 57 33 Fax ++(49) 6104 66 57 34
www.ontosverlag.com

ISBN 3-937202-71-4

2005

Printed on acid-free paper
ISO-Norm 970-6

Printed in Germany.

021406 - 2909 P8

CONTENTS

8   Contents

PREFACE

Without doubt Richard Rorty is one of the most honored, famous and dispu-
ted philosophers of our days. Interest in his inspiring and provoking thoughts
is taken beyond academic circles of philosophy. I would like to emphasize
three features of his writings. Firstly, he pursues a combination of the Anglo-
Saxon tradition of analytic philosophy and continental philosophy. Secondly,
his wide-ranging fields of interest embrace theoretical philosophy as well as
practical, political and cultural philosophy. Thirdly, he aims at making academic philosophy accessible to the public.

The department of philosophy at the University of Münster invited Richard Rorty to the *8. Münstersche Vorlesungen zur Philosophie*. Richard Rorty presented his lecture to a public audience on 26th of May 2004. Papers on Rorty's
philosophy, which were written by students and faculty of the philosophy department, were discussed intensively on the following day. The present volume contains Richard Rorty's public lecture „The Brain as Hardware, Culture
as Software", an additional short text entitled „Philosophy-Envy", the papers
of the working groups and Richard Rorty's responses to them. In view of the
wide range of topics discussed, the subtitle of the volume „His Philosophy
Under Discussion" is not an unsuitable exaggeration. Richard Rorty commen-
ted on the students' papers, and his clarifying responses may stimulate the
reader of this volume to precise or revise her understanding of Rorty's philosophy.

I should like to thank all the participants in the colloquium. Firstly, I owe
gratitude to Richard Rorty who got intensively involved in discussions with
the students and who openly dealt with their theses and arguments. Additionally, I have to thank him for supplying his texts to us, and especially for putting his responses in writing. Secondly, I am grateful to the working groups
(students and colleagues of the department of philosophy) who prepared highly interesting papers on a wide range of topics and who spent much time in
discussing Richard Rorty's thoughts.

I am grateful to Stefan Heßbrüggen who helped me with the organization of the working groups and the colloquium. I am grateful to David P. Schweikard who revised the texts. I am grateful to Judith Enge, Katharina Kleinewillinghöfer, and Arne Grießer who actively ensured the successful course of the colloquium.

The *Münstersche Vorlesungen zur Philosophie* differs from other colloquia and conferences since students write and present their own papers. To get funding for this kind of conference has been difficult. The department of philosophy at the University of Münster appreciates that the ontos verlag expressed willingness to sponsor the *Münstersche Vorlesungen zur Philosophie* from now on. I sincerely would like to thank the ontos verlag for generous funding of the present colloquium and this publication.

Münster, December 2004   *Andreas Vieth*

LIST OF ABBREVIATIONS
OF RICHARD RORTY'S PUBLICATIONS

AM   »Die Armen sind die große Mehrheit«, in: *Deutsche Zeitschrift für Philosophie* 46, 1998, p. 983-990.

AOC   *Achieving Our Country, Leftist Thought in Twentieth Century America*, Cambridge: Harvard Univ. Pr., 1998.

AW   »Antiskeptical Weapons: Michael Williams Versus Donald Davidson«, in: TP, p. 153-163.

BRA   »Beyond Realism and Anti-Realism«, in: *Wo Steht die Analytische Philosophie heute?*, ed. by Richard Heinrich and Ludwig Nagl, Vienna: R. Oldenbourg Verlag, 1986, p. 103-115.

CIS   *Contingency, Irony, and Solidarity*, Cambridge: Cambridge Univ. Pr., 1989.

CL   »The Contingency of Language«, in: CIS, p. 3-22.

CLC   »The Contingency of a Liberal Community«, in: CIS, p. 44-69.

CP   *Consequences of Pragmatism, Essays 1972-1980*, Minneapolis: Univ. of Minnesota Pr., 1982.

CS   »The Contingency of Selfhood«, in: CIS, p. 23-43.

CTT   »Charles Taylor on Truth«, in: TP, p. 84-97.

DDI   »Daniel Dennett on Intrinsicality«, in: TP, p. 98-121.

DM   »Dewey's Metaphysics«, in: CP, p. 72-89.

EMF   »Erwiderung auf Friederike Müller-Friemauth«, in: HS, p. 259-263.

ETS   »Erwiderung auf Thomas Schäfer«, in: HS, p. 194-200.

HS   *Hinter den Spiegeln. Beiträge zur Philosophie Richard Rortys*, ed. by Thomas Schäfer, Udo Tietz and Rüdiger Zill, Frankfurt am Main: Suhrkamp, 2001, p. 259-263.

HSE   *Hoffnung statt Erkenntnis, Eine Einführung in die pragmatische Philosophie*, Vienna: Passagen-Verlag, 1994.

IR   »Inquiry as Recontextualization«, in: ORT, p. 93-110.

ITGI   »Is Truth a Goal of Inquiry? Donald Davidson Versus Crispin
        Wright«, in: TP, p. 19-42.
KOZ   *Eine Kultur ohne Zentrum*, Stuttgart: Reclam, 1993.
NRP   »Non-Reductive Physicalism«, in: ORT, p. 113-125.
NSNK   »Is Natural Science a Natural Kind?«, in: ORT, p. 46-62.
ORT   *Objectivity, Relativism, and Truth, Philosophical Papers, Vol. 1*, Cambridge:
        Cambridge Univ. Pr., 1991.
PDT   »Pragmatism, Davidson and Truth«, in: ORT, p. 126-150.
PILH   »Private Irony and Liberal Hope«, in: CIS, p. 73-95.
PRM   »Hilary Putnam and the Relativist Menace«, in: TP, p. 43-62.
RCD   »Rationality and Cultural Difference«, in: TP, p. 186-201.
S   »Solidarity«, in: CIS, p. 189-198.
SDW   »›Sieben Dollar sind zu wenig.‹ Weshalb die Linke sich nicht
        globalisieren kann«, in: *Frankfurter Rundschau*, 1. August 2000, p. 19.
SO   »Solidarity or Objectivitiy?«, in: ORT, p. 21-34.
SRR   »John Searle on Realism and Relativism«, in: TP, p. 63-83.
TP   *Truth and Progress, Philosophical Papers, Vol. 3*, Cambridge: Cambridge
        Univ. Pr., 1998.
UT   »Universality and Truth«, in: *Rorty and His Critics*, ed. by Robert B.
        Brandom, Oxford: Blackwell, 2000, p. 1-31.
WSW   »Eine Welt ohne Substanz oder Wesen«, in: HSE, p. 37-66.
WWL   »The World Well Lost«, in: *The Journal of Philosophy* 69, 1972, p. 649-
        665 (reprinted in CP, p. 3-18).

THE BRAIN AS HARDWARE, CULTURE AS SOFTWARE *

Richard Rorty

1 Neo-Carnapians vs. Neo-Wittgensteinians: Chomsky vs. Davidson

For the last fifty years or so there has been a struggle going on between the heirs of Carnap's »unified science« movement and the followers of the later Wittgenstein. The differences between these two kinds of philosophers are best grasped, nowadays, by contrasting their attitudes toward cognitive science.

The Carnapians see the acknowledged impossibility of the sort of behavioristic reductionism that Carnap once hoped to achieve as having left us with a problem about the place of intentionality in a world of physical particles. But many of them regard that problem as having finally been solved in a non-reductionistic way, thanks to »the computational revolution«. That revolution, Jerry Fodor tells us, was made possible because »computers showed us how to connect semantics with causal properties of symbols«.[1] Thinking about computers helped us realize that symbols could become incarnate as neural states, and thereby exert causal power. Fodor sees this revolution as a great intellectual breakthrough, giving us an insight into how the mind works that was previously unavailable.

Philosophers of mind and language who are skeptical about this revolution, such as Davidson, Brandom and Descombes, are not troubled by the irreducibility of the intentional. Following Wittgenstein's lead, they think the irreducibility of one vocabulary to another presents no more problems than the

*   First published in *Inquiry* 47 (No. 3), 2004, pp. 219-235.
1   Fodor 1989, p. 18.

unsubstitutability of one tool for another. Nor do they think of the mind as a mechanism whose workings cognitive scientists can study. They agree that the brain is such a mechanism, but they do not think it useful to identify the mind with the brain.

These neo-Wittgensteinians urge us to drop what Ryle called »Descartes' para-mechanical hypothesis«, rather than to reinterpret it in physicalist terms by treating brain states as representations. The heirs of Wittgenstein would like to get rid of the whole idea of internal representations, and of mechanisms that produce such representations. Whereas the neo-Carnapians regard mind and language as things that can be understood by taking them apart and seeing how their parts gear in with one another and with features of the organism's environment, the neo-Wittgensteinians see them as social skills. Davidson, for example, says that, although a theory of meaning must describe what an interpreter can do, there is no reason to think that »some mechanism in the interpreter must correspond to the theory«.[2]

Chomsky's comment on that claim is that »for anyone approaching these problems from the standpoint of the natural sciences« Davidson's way of thinking is »utterly wrongheaded«.[3] A similar skepticism about underlying mechanisms would, he points out, have inhibited the development of chemistry. Just as Dalton and Mendelejev enabled us to see mechanical interactions between atoms behind the ability of elements to combine into compounds, so cognitive science will enable us to see mechanical interactions between nerve cells behind the exercise of social skills. For Chomsky, philosophers like Quine, Davidson and Dummett are Canute figures, trying to hold back a rising tide of established empirical results.

These results include, he claims, the discovery that »an initial state of the language faculty incorporates certain general principles of language structure, including phonetic and semantic principles«.[4] Ever since he published *Cartesian linguistics*, some twenty-five years ago, Chomsky has made clear his distaste for Wittgensteinian anti-Cartesianism – and in particular for the idea that we can be content to think of language simply as a teachable skill, rather that as a

---

2   Davidson 1986, p. 438.
3   Chomsky 2000, p. 56.
4   Ibid., p. 60.

generative procedure.[5] Whereas Ryle thought that it was only »Descartes' myth« that the study of what he called »qualities of intellect and character« could be a study of mechanisms, Chomsky thinks that Descartes and Locke pointed us in the right direction. He is as sure that their analogies between physical and mental atoms put philosophy on the right track as Quine was that they put it on the wrong one. Chomsky has helped deepen and widen the division between the philosophers who agree with Ryle and Wittgenstein that the »idea idea« has outlived its usefulness and those who do not.

Chomsky is caustic about Davidson's claim that Quine »saved philosophy of language as a serious subject« by getting rid of the analytic-synthetic distinction. That distinction, Chomsky says, is taken for granted by »virtually everyone who works in descriptive semantics«. As he writes:

> One would be hard put to find studies of language that do not assign structures and describe the meaning of *kill, so*, etc., in such a way that there is a qualitative distinction – determined by the language itself – between the sentences »John killed Bill, so Bill is dead« and John killed Bill, so John is dead«.[6]

Chomsky says that we need the distinction between what is »determined by the language itself« and what is not in order to explain such phenomena of language-learning as that »each child knows the relevant difference between ›who did John see Bill with?‹ and ›who did John see Bill and?‹« Since, as he says, »children do not ... produce ›who did John see Bill and?‹, then to be informed by their parents that this is not the way it is done«, the only explanation available is the innate structure of the language faculty.[7]

Chomsky's argument here depends on the assumption that the absence of certain behavior is as good an explanandum as its presence. But this is as if we asked for an explanation of why no child continues the sequence »2, 4, 6, 8«, after reaching triple digits, with »104, 108, 112«, and of why no correction or instruction by parents is necessary to insure that the child stays on track. The Chomskian explanation would presumably be that an innate mechanism

5   For this contrast, see Chomsky 2000, p. 50.
6   Ibid., p. 47.
7   Ibid., p. 56.

is at work. For philosophers like Davidson, this is a »dormitive power« explanation of a non-event.

The standoff between Davidson and Chomsky over these matters is
clearest when Chomsky criticizes Davidson's attempt to »erase the boundary
between knowing a language and knowing our way around the world generally.« This erasure would give empirical inquiry into language no foothold, for it
would make a theory of language-learning what Chomsky calls »a theory of
everything«. »The proper conclusion«, he continues,

> is not that we must abandon concepts of language that can be produc-
> tively studied [such as Chomsky's own concept of »a internal representa-
> tion of a generative procedure«[8]] but that the topic of successful com-
> munication in the actual world of experience is far too complex and
> obscure to merit attention in empirical inquiry.[9]

Chomsky thinks that the sort of common-sense explanation of how children
learn language with which Davidson is content will not do for scientific purposes, because »Reference to ›misuse of language‹, to ›norms‹, to ›communities‹, and so on ... require[s] much more care than is taken. These concepts are
obscure, and it is not clear that they are of any use for inquiry into language
and human behavior«.[10] In passages such as this, Chomsky shows himself the
true heir of Carnap. Carnap too would have found the notion of »norm«
obscure, and unsuitable for purposes of scientific inquiry. But for Wittgensteinians to make a concept clear is simply to become familiar with the use of
a linguistic expression. For them, the use of »interiorization of social norms«
is no more problematic than the use of »internal representation of a generative procedure«, and perhaps less so.

From a Wittgensteinian perspective, the approach taken by Chomsky
and his fellow cognitive scientists looks like that taken by the man who sear-
ches for his missing keys under the lamp-post, not because he dropped them
near there but because the light is better. What Chomsky calls »the standpoint
of the natural sciences« is simply the habit of looking for micro-mechanisms

8   Ibid., p. 69.
9   Ibid., p. 70.
10   Ibid., p. 72.

behind macroscropic behavior. The claim that adopting this standpoint will always pay off looks to Wittgensteinians like Carnapian dogmatism.

Consider, for example, Chomsky's claim that there is »a fixed biological-ly-determined function that maps evidence available into acquired knowledge, uniformly for all languages«.[11] It hard to see this as an empirical result, since it is hard to think what could disconfirm it. It is uncontroversial that organisms that can learn languages have this ability because they have different neural layouts than other organisms. The layouts, to be sure, are biologically de-termined. But in what sense can a *function* be so determined?

To say that a mechanism embodies a function is just to say that its beha-vior can usefully be described in terms of a certain specifiable relation bet-ween input and output. Nobody can specify any such relation between the in-puts provided by language-teaching adults and the outputs provided by a language-learning child, because they are too various. It would be like trying to specify a relation between the events that occur in the course of learning to ride a bicycle and those that are the actions of the accomplished bicyclist.

But, Chomsky tells us, there is a function that, rather than mapping in-puts onto outputs, maps inputs into something called »acquired knowledge«. Well, the bicyclist too has acquired some knowledge. Should we say that he has acquired it thanks to a biologically-determined function that maps the events of his early, tentative, abortive, rides onto a set of internal representa-tions whose possession is a necessary condition of his newly-acquired ability? We could, but what would count as confirming the existence of such a media-ting entity, in between the learning events and the actions which produce suc-cessful bicycle rides?

Considerations such as this led Wittgenstein to end *Philosophical Investiga-tions* and Ryle to end *The concept of mind* with doubts about psychology as a dis-cipline. Both philosophers doubted that there would ever be a payoff from postulating mediating »psychologically real states« between observable behavi-or and neural micro-layouts – the sort of payoff in ability to predict and con-trol that we got from postulating unobservable physical particles. Wittgen-stein said that the idea that »psychology treats of processes in the psychical sphere, as does physics in the physical« was a »misleading parallel«,[12] and that

11   Ibid., p. 53.
12   Wittgenstein 1958, I, sec. 571.

»the confusion and barrenness of psychology is not to be explained by calling it a ›young science‹«[13]. Contemporary Wittgensteinians have similar sentiments about contemporary cognitive science.

It is one thing to say that Chomskian linguistics, and the other academic specialities that bill themselves as parts of »cognitive science«, are respectable disciplines – arenas in which very bright people engage in spirited debates with one another. It is another thing to say that these disciplines have contributed to our knowledge. Many equally respectable disciplines have flourished and decayed without leaving such contributions behind them. Fifteenth century Aristotelianism, seventeenth century hermeticism, and twentieth century logical empiricism are familiar examples.

Wittgensteinians think that it is an open question whether cognitive science will go down in history as a successful attempt to bring the procedures of natural science to bear on the study of mind and language or as yet another attempt to set philosophy on the secure path of a science – one that eventually collapsed, like all the others, of its own weight. They suspect that cognitive science may never be able to disentangle itself from philosophy in the way that chemistry did – by exhibiting its ability to spin off new technologies. Whereas the fans of cognitive science view the Wittgensteinians as dogmatic behaviorists, the Wittgensteinians criticize the Chomskians in the same terms as Bacon criticized late scholasticism. They think of Chomsky and Fodor in the same way that he thought of Occam and Scotus: all their beautiful theories and subtle arguments cannot be brought to bear on practice. They are building mechanisms in the air.

2   COMPOSITIONALITY: FODOR VS. BRANDOM

Fodor tries to break through the impasse by arguing that if the Wittgensteinians are to do more than vent quasi-behaviorist prejudices, they must come up with some theory of their own about the way in which language works. All they can produce, he suspects, is »semantic holism«, the doctrine

---

13   Ibid., I, sec. 232

that »the meaning of an expression is constituted by all of its inferential relations, hence by all of its role in a language«.[14]

That doctrine is put forward implicitly by Davidson and explicitly by
Brandom. Since the study of the roles of expressions in languages is the study
of what Chomsky calls »successful communication in the actual world of experience«, and since holists cannot easily distinguish between knowing a language and knowing one's way about in the world generally, this study cannot
avoid becoming what Chomsky dismissively calls a »theory of everything«. So
semantics cannot be the sort of discipline that sustains an analogy with chemistry, and perhaps cannot be a discipline at all. That is why Davidson and
Brandom offer no research programs for eager young cognitive scientists to
carry out, and why they seem to Chomsky like obstructionist Luddites. It is
also why Brandom sees no point in retaining the old Carnapian distinction
between semantics and pragmatics.[15]

Fodor thinks that there is a decisive reply to the semantic holists, one
that leaves the Chomskians in possession of the field. It is that language is
compositional: »the meaning of syntactically complex expressions is a function of their syntactic structure together with the meaning of their syntactic
constituents«.[16] Since »meanings are compositional but inferential roles are
not compositional, meanings can't be inferential roles«.[17] Fodor spells out the
point as follows:

> The meaning of the phrase ›brown cow‹ ... depends on the meanings of
> ›brown‹ and ›cow‹ together with its syntax ... But now, prima facie, the in-
> ferential role of brown cow depends not only on the inferential role of
> ›brown‹ and the inferential role of ›cow‹ but also on *what you happen to
> believe about brown cows*. So, unlike meaning, inferential role is, in the gene-
> ral case, not compositional.[18]

At this point in the argument, Wittgensteinians will say that if there were such
things as meanings, languages would indeed be compositional, but that Quine

14   Fodor 1994, p. 153.
15   See Brandom 1994, p. 592.
16   Ibid., p. 146.
17   Ibid., p. 147.
18   Ibid., pp. 147-148.

and Davidson have given us good reason to think that there are not. They see no reason to postulate relations between mental or linguistic atoms called »meanings« or »concepts« or »representations« in order to explain the social skills of language-learning organisms. To think that there is a feature called »sameness of meaning« to be detected within the conversational flux is to insist on a pre-Quinean distinction between language and fact that serves no purpose except to keep cognitive scientists employed. Fodor describes this Wittgensteinian line of argument as

> a well-greased, and well-traveled slippery slope: having arrived at the bottom, one finds oneself accepting such prima facie outlandish doctrines as that no two people ever share a belief, that there is no such relation as translation; that no two people ever mean the same thing by what they say; that no two time slices of the same person ever mean the same thing by what they say; that no one can ever change his mind; that no statements, or beliefs, can ever be contradicted (to say nothing of refuted), and so forth. It is a moot question how to get the goodness out of inferential role semantics without paying this extravagant price.[19]

In response, Wittgensteinians make the Rylean point that we can describe two people as having the same thing – for example, the same build or the same outlook – without being able to specify criteria of sameness. Ryle noted that there is an everyday sense in which many people have the same build and the same outlook, and another, equally useful, sense in which no two people have either. Similarly, the utility of the everyday sense of »means the same« and »believes the same« should not make us reject the point that Descombes approvingly quotes from Sartre: »whenever I form a sentence its meaning escapes me, is stolen from me; meanings are changed for everyone by each speaker and each day; the meanings of the very words in my mouth are changed by others«.[20] Brandom echoes this when he says »A word – ›dog‹, ›stupid‹, ›Republican‹ – has a different significance in my mouth than it does in yours, be-

19   Ibid., p. 143.
20   Descombes 2001, p. 247.

cause and insofar as what follows from its being applicable, its consequences of application, differ for me, in virtue of my different collateral beliefs«.[21]

Fodor insists that the Achilles heel of the Wittgensteinians is the productivity of natural languages, a property that can only be explained by compositionality. He defines productivity, roughly, as the ability to express an openended set of propositions – well-formed strings of potentially infinite length. But Wittgensteinians will reply that it is only if we are already thinking of languages as generative mechanisms that we shall think of them as having any such ability. If we follow Davidson in denying the need for »portable interpreting machines set to grind out the meaning of arbitrary utterances« we shall not. For those who think of knowing a language as a skill, the infinite productivity that Fodor cites will seem as irrelevant as the potentially infinite variety of maneuvers that the experienced bicyclist is able to execute.

»Productivity«, Fodor says, »is the property that a system has when it has an infinite number of syntactically and semantically distinct symbols.«[22] But from a Wittgensteinian perspective that is a good reason to deny that what speakers of a natural language have is such a system. If one abstracts out an abstract entity called »English« from the conversational interchanges of various organisms, one can say, as Fodor does, that »English contains the openended sequence of nonsynonomous expressions: ›missile shield‹, ›anti-missile shield‹, ›anti-anti-missile-shield-shield‹ ... and so forth«. But that is like saying that an abstract entity called »arithmetic« contains such an open-ended sequence. Abstract entities can have properties that organisms cannot. In particular, they can contain infinite numbers of things. Skills such as speaking English or riding a bicycle contain neither finite nor infinite numbers of things.

---

21   Brandom 1994, p. 587. See also p. 509: »... a sentence in one person's mouth does not typically have the same significance as that same sentence emerging from another person's mouth, even where there is as much sharing of the language and as much mutual understanding as one likes. The fundamental reason is the kind of things claims and concepts are.« As I remark below, Brandom and Descombes take concepts to be more like people than like atoms, in that they have histories but not natures.

22   Fodor 2002, p. 1.

3   DETERMINATE BEING

Another way in which Fodor formulates the issue between the Carnapians
and the Wittgensteinians is by contrasting »meaning realists« – people who
think that »there are facts about meaning, and that they are suitable objects of
scientific inquiry« – with those who think that »meaning arises from our practices of interpretation, so that there no more needs to be a single right answer
to ›what does ›pinochle‹ mean?‹ than there is to ›what does *Hamlet* mean?‹«
Wittgensteinians, he says, think that »trying for a science of meaning would be
silly; like trying for a science of games. Or of Tuesdays.«[23]

Fodor deplores what he calls »sympathy with this Wittgenstein-Good-
man-Kuhn-Derrida sort of picture«, and prays to God that »no miasmal mist
from Harvard has seeped up [sic] the Charles to MIT«.[24] He associates this
miasma with what he calls »linguistic idealism,« a view he attributes to philosophers »like Rorty, Putnam, Kuhn and Derrida«.[25] That sort of philosopher
thinks that meaning realism is as pointless as, recurring to Ryle's examples,
build realism or outlook realism.

Quine initiated the Harvard-based assault on meaning realism by
claiming that beliefs and meanings could never be fitted into a physicalistic
world view, precisely because the indeterminacy of intentional ascription
meant that there is no way to tell whether two people mean the same thing by
the same words, or share the same belief. Starting from the claim that there is
no entity without identity, Quine concluded that beliefs and meanings have
no place in any world-picture that »limns the true and ultimate structure of
reality«.

Fodor argues that since beliefs and meanings *need* to be given such a
place, and since Quine was right that there can be no entity without identity,
we must be meaning realists. Brandom, by contrast, sees no need either to insist that there is a single right answer to the question »what does ›pinochle‹
mean?« or to follow Quine in inferring from the lack of such an answer to the
claim that beliefs and meanings are somehow not on an ontological par with

23   Fodor 2000a, p. 22.
24   Fodor 2000b.
25   Fodor 2002, pp. 22-23.

electrons and neurons. Davidson's account of linguistic competence in »A nice derangement of epitaphs« is of a piece with Brandom's view that knowing the content of an assertion is a matter of determining its current place in some particular game of giving and asking for reasons. For both philosophers, social skills of the sort required to have intelligent conversations do not require the application of criteria for sameness of meaning or of belief.

The three-cornered dialectic between Fodor, Quine and the Wittgensteinians can be summarized by saying that Fodor and Quine agree that the only beings that exist are those for which there are context-free criteria of identity, whereas Davidson and Brandom do not. But a more illuminating way of describing this standoff is provided by the terminology used by Cornelius Castoriadis and, more recently, by Vincent Descombes. Descombes says that Castoriadis criticized

> an intractable prejudice of philosophers and of all those whom they (often unknowingly) inspire: that everything that exists exists in a determinate form. Everything that exists is precise, determined, and apprehensible. If by chance something exhibits indetermination, laziness, or vagueness, then that thing has shown itself to be, if not utterly illusory, at least of inferior status.[26]

For Descombes, the trouble with Fodor, Quine and others who think that entity requires identity is that they succumb to what he calls »the illusion of a general metaphysics«. Such a metaphysics, he says

> would have to take up unity and plurality, identity and difference, the individual and relations, all without taking any particular domain into consideration. In particular, it would have to make clear how the words »being« and »identity« are to be understood before philosophical inquiry is divided into »regional ontologies«, including the ontology of nature and the ontology of mind. ... [But] how can one inquire into conditions of identity without taking into account the type of things one seeks to identify?[27]

26 Descombes 2001, p. 240.
27 Ibid., p. 241.

Here Descombes makes a point that is also made by Brandom. Descombes says that »the concept ›thing‹ is not meant to be applied in an exercise of enumeration«. Brandom says that

> establishing a criterion of identity is not only sufficient for countability; it is necessary as well. Unsortalized ›things‹ or ›objects‹ cannot be counted. There is no answer to the question how many things there are in this room; there is one number of books, another of molecules, another of atoms, another of subatomic particles ... Counting is intelligible only by reference to a sortal concept.«[28]

But the fact that only what has been sorted out can be counted does not entail that all sortals pick out sets of countable items. As Descombes points out, the fact that one does not begin to know how to answer the question »How many representations are there in Gericault's painting *The raft of the Medusa?*« is not because representations are fuzzier than other things, but because unsortalized representations are as bad as unsortalized things. So to answer the ›how many?‹ question, Descombes says, »one would have to be able to enumerate the things represented in the painting«.[29]

The same problem, he points out, arises in the case of a brain. Suppose that someone who believes that brains contain representational states wants to enumerate the representations present in the visual cortex of a brain attached to an eye that is focused on an approaching predator. The number she will come up with will depend upon whether she treats the brain as representing colors, or shades of colors, or patterns of colors, or middle-sized physical objects, or light waves, or environmental dangers, or chemical changes in the retina. To say that the brain is a computational device is not yet to decide which of many input-output functions the device is programmed to run. There are as many such functions as there are alternative descriptions of its environment and of its behavior. To be a meaning realist is to hold that one such function is the right one. But it is dubious that empirical evidence can decide between all those descriptions. That would be like gathe-

28   Brandom 1994, p. 438.
29   Descombes 2001, p. 241.

ring empirical evidence in the hope of deciding whether my laptop is currently processing ones and zeros, or words, or thoughts.

Seen from the Descombes-Brandom angle, the Quinean idea that
meanings have a second-rate ontological status because an indefinitely large
number of different translation manuals would do equal justice to the behavioral evidence is like saying that there is not really such a thing as visual perception because an indefinitely large number of input-output functions would
do equal justice to observed correlations between events in the visual cortex
and events in the organism's environment. The impulse to infer from the
existence of alternative descriptions to ontological second-rateness is found
only in those who are subject to what Descombes calls »the illusion of a general metaphysics«.

So the Wittgensteinian response to Quine's doctrine of the indeterminacy of translation is to deny that there is anything especially problematic
about language, or, more generally, about the intentional. As Chomsky was,
ironically enough, the first to argue, the indeterminacy of translation (and of
intentional ascription) is not interestingly different from the ordinary under-
determination of theory by evidence. Such under-determination is no more
puzzling than the familiar fact that if you have found it useful to have two distinct vocabularies available for describing the same chunk of space-time it is
unlikely that you can straightforwardly infer from an assertion formulated in
the one to an assertion formulated in the other. For if such inferences were
sufficiently common, the two vocabularies would long since have collapsed
into one another.

Philosophers who, like myself, get their kicks from inhaling the Wittgen-
stein-Goodman-Kuhn-Derrida miasma claim to know quite well why »rabbit«
translates »Gavagai« better than »rabbit-stage«. We are confident that it has
nothing to do with inspecting two entities called »meanings« and ticking off
their resemblances and dissimilarities. It has everything to do with the relative
ease of acquisition of the social skills promoted by bilingualism. Analogously,
we can see the utility of sometimes treating the organism as responding to vi-
sually presented middle-sized physical objects, sometimes to aesthetic values,
and sometimes to light waves, without worrying about what it is »really« responding to. The latter question seems to us as bad as the question of what
Hamlet is *really* about, or of whether the »real« subject of *Winnie the Pooh*, is

child abuse, or the self-consuming character of literary artifacts, or the collap-
se of late capitalism.[30] The multiplicity of input-output functions available for
describing the same state of a computer parallels the multiplicity of contexts
into which Frederick Crews puts A. A. Milne's text.

If cognitive scientists come to agree on which such function to select, it
is presumably because they agree that the purposes of their discipline – the
prediction and control of human and animal behavior – are best served by
this choice. But Wittgensteinians doubt that such agreement will ever be reached. Their hesitancy to adopt what Chomsky calls »the standard methods of
the natural sciences« and to attribute semantic properties to brain states, is
due to their doubt that doing so will ever be useful for purposes of prediction
and control. The issue is neither ontological nor methodological but practical.
You do not get to claim the prerogatives of a natural science simply by per-
forming experiments and formulating hypotheses to explain their results.
Even the alchemists could do that. To be recognized as such a science you
have to make some concrete contributions to what Bacon called »the improvement of man's estate«.

Wittgensteinians doubt that postulating »a fixed biologically-determined
function that maps evidence available into acquired knowledge, uniformly for
all languages« will let us learn more languages faster, or that it will do much to
explain why some people have so much trouble learning any foreign language.
On the other hand, they are quite willing to predict that someday both ped-
agogy and therapy will be greatly improved by our ability to tweak neurons.
For Wittgensteinians are as good physicalists as Carnapians. They are equally
committed to the view that you cannot alter somebody's psychological state
without altering – somewhere, somehow – her brain state. What they doubt is
that there is a profitable level of inquiry in between folk psychology and
neurology – whether profitable tweaking will be facilitated by the discovery of
what is »psychologically real«.

30   See Crews 2001.

4 DESCOMBES ON THE LOCATION OF THE MIND

One of the important contributions that Descombes has made to the current debate is to tie it in with the fact that, long before the computational revolution, philosophers were disagreeing about what sort of thing the mind is, and, more specifically, about where it is. They were, Descombes says, split on whether the mind is »within or without«:

> Within, according to the mentalist heirs of Descartes, Locke, Hume and Maine de Brian and among whom one can also place the phenomenologists and the cognitivists. Without, according to the philosophers of objective mind and the public use of signs, for example Peirce and Wittgenstein.[31]

This contrast between Descartes, Locke and Hume on the one hand and Peirce and Wittgenstein on the other highlights another similarity between Descombes and Brandom. Brandom views Wittgenstein as a precursor of his own inferentialist, »social practice«, approach to mind and language, the approach that he opposes to the representationalism of Locke and Hume. He and Descombes are in rough agreement about which philosophers were the good guys.

The biggest difference between Descombes' and Brandom's strategies is that Descombes divides the great dead philosophers into sheep and goats by invoking his internalist-externalist distinction. He says that one of the principal aims of *The mind's provisions* will be to argue for externalism – to show that internalism (also known as »the classical philosophy of the subject«) is wrong in holding that a thought is mental because inside the skull, whereas a book, being outside, is merely physical. A book, like a nation, counts as a bit of what Hegel called *objective Geist* and both are examples of what Peirce called »a sign«.

This way of putting the matter leads Descombes to conclude, in his final chapter, that if cognitive science ever does get beyond the drum-beating stage

---

31 Descombes 2001, p. 2.

it would still be »unable to tell us about the mind, i. e., about thoughts«. The reason for this inability, Descombes says, is that

> mental vocabulary is deeply historical, which is another way of saying that there are historical conditions of meaning. A subject's words and thoughts have the meaning that they must be given in his world and cannot be disassociated from that world ... The world that must be known in order to know what the subject thinks is not just a natural world ... [I]t is a cultural world, one that contains institutions like the calendar, money, banks, and the game of chess.[32]

I think that Descombes could make his point equally well if he did not ask us to take sides on the internalism-externalism question, but instead suggested that we view »the mind« as a term that has been used both to describe something internal – whatever it is that each adult human has that enables him to take part in such distinctively human activities as playing chess and depositing money in banks – and something external, namely the aggregate of such activities. This aggregate can usefully be described as »objective Spirit« or, more simply, as »culture«, but calling it »mind« seems to me unnecessarily paradoxical.

Descombes' main point is that knowing about the brain is unlikely to help us understand anything about culture, and conversely. That thesis is both true and important. It is indeed unlikely that there will ever be the sort of »unity of knowledge« that Carnap (and, nowadays, E. O. Wilson and other sociobiologists) hope for. But I would prefer to evade Descombes' question »where is the mind located?« by saying that two quite different things have, confusingly, been designated by that term. One is the hard-wiring of the anthropoid brain and the other is the set of social skills that we call »culture«. »Mind« in the solipsistic, Cartesian, inside-the-skull sense is, indeed the brain – just as the cognitive scientists insist. »Mind« in the sense of objective spirit, the sense in which books and paintings are mental entities, is obviously not the brain. It is the social world in which we find calendars and chessboards.

This Solomonic strategy of cutting the mind in two and giving a half to each claimant may seem too quick and dirty a way of dealing with the debates

32   Descombes 2001, p. 244.

currently raging in philosophy of mind and language. But I shall try to illustrate its advantages by showing how nicely the distinction between brain and culture parallels that between hardware and software.

5 BRAIN AS HARDWARE, CULTURE AS SOFTWARE

To illustrate the relevance of that distinction, consider the following fiction: In the twenty-fourth century, everybody owns a computer which is to today's models as they are to Babbage's calculating engine. Everybody carries around exactly the same model, an exact replica of a prototype that appeared two hundred years earlier, and that has been robotically duplicated in enormous quantities and at trivial cost ever since. If your computer begins to go bad, you throw it away and pick up a new one exactly like it. Because of the original manufacturer's monopolistic greed, if you try to open up your computer it self-destructs, and if you try to get into the robotic assembly line the robots kill you. Though software gets better and better every year, hardware remains completely unchanged. Nobody in the twenty-fourth century has any idea how the computers work, of what goes on inside the black boxes.

But one day it becomes clear that the self-destruct mechanism has ceased to function on the most recently produced computers. So people start tearing their computers apart and doing reverse engineering. They discover that it is all done with 1's and 0's. The crucial gimmick is that both program instructions and data take the form of binary numbers. They proceed to reconstruct the various levels of programming language that were built into the machine's operating system. Now, they say, the mystery of how the gadget works has been solved: we know all there is to be known about hardware. Whether this knowledge will be of any use when developing new software, however, remains to be seen.

The analogy I want to draw is obvious. Culture is to software as the brain is to hardware. The brain has long been a black box, but with the help of nanotechnology we may someday be able to pick it apart, axon by axon, and say »Aha, the gimmick is ...«. This will probably produce new pedagogical techniques and new therapies. But it is not at all clear that it will do anything for »the unity of knowledge«. We already knew that our brains could be pro-

grammed to do a lot of different things, just as the computer users in my fiction knew that their computers could. Discovering the micro-structural details
of the brain might enable us to do different things with it than we had previously done, or it might not, just as further information about hardware
design might or might not facilitate the production of improved software. But
whether it does or not, it is hard to see that why we would begin to see the relation between the natural sciences and the human sciences in a new way.

The main reason for thinking that the *Natur-Geist* distinction will remain
as important as it has always been is that intentional ascription is holistic:
beliefs cannot be individuated in such a way as to correlate with neural states.
Convincing arguments for this thesis have been offered by, among others,
Davidson, Arthur Collins, Lynn Baker, and Helen Steward. They have shown
why we cannot hope to map *beliefs* onto neural states, though such mapping
might work for, for example, mental images, or surges of lust. If there is
nothing interesting to be discovered about how changes in belief are related
to neurological mechanisms, it is hard to see how studies of what Chomsky
calls »the brain/mind« can be expected to interact with studies of culture.

This point helps one see what is wrong with Chomsky's analogy with
chemistry. Dalton and Mendelejev helped us see how macrostructure fitted
together with microstructure. The exaltation produced by such macro-micro
correlations produced Carnap's »unity of science« initiative. *But the hardware-
software and the brain-culture relations are not micro-macro relations. They are examples of
the relation between a tool and its manifold uses.*

It is sometimes suggested that the discovery of how the brain works will
tie in with evolutionary biology so as to enable us to understand better what
our brain has been tailored to do, and thus to understand »human nature«
better. But the analogy between biological evolution and software development suggests that what the brain was originally tailored to do may be irrelevant to what it is currently being used for. The fact that the first software
breakthroughs were in the area of missile targeting, and of information search
and retrieval, tells us nothing in particular about what present-day computers
are good for. The fact that some early stages in the evolution of the human
brain were dictated by the needs of hunter-gatherers tells us equally little
about what to do with the resulting product.

Steven Pinker tells us that »The mind is a system of organs of computation, designed by natural selection to solve the kinds of problems our ancestors faced in their foraging way of life«.[33] Descombes would presumably reply that that is true of the brain but not of the mind. I would urge, however, that Pinker's sentence is misleading even if we substitute »brain« for »mind« as its subject. It is misleading for the same reason that it would be misleading to say that my laptop, which I use only for word processing, was designed to track missiles and comb data bases. Accounts of what the original designers of tools had in mind make little difference to the uses to which we put those tools.

This pragmatic attitude is the one that Wittgensteinians adopt when confronted with books like Pinker's and Wilson's, which tell us that linguistics, cognitive psychology, and evolutionary biology are conspiring to change the human self-image. These books tell us that what we had previously thought to be cultural will turn out to be biological. But this claim would sound convincing only if we come to think that evolution has created a brain that unfortunately cannot be programmed in a certain way – a brain so constructed that certain input-output functions cannot be realized by it. To acknowledge the hegemony of the biological would be to admit that some seemingly promising cultural initiative should not be attempted, because biology blocks it.

It is hard to imagine what the argument for such blockage would look like. For it would amount to saying: do not even try to modify our social practices in the proposed way, because we know in advance that it will not work. We know that the experiment should not be tried, because it is foredoomed. This would be analogous to saying »Stop trying to transmute base metals into gold, for Dalton and Mendelejev have shown why this will never happen.« But presumably the only way in which a cognitive scientist like Pinker or Wilson could back up such an injunction would be to show, on physiological grounds, that a certain belief cannot be held or that a certain desire could not be had. This would be hard, not only because of the philosophical arguments against the cerebral localizability of intentional states that I mentioned earlier, but because if a belief really could never be held, nobody would ever have been able to propose that it be propagated.

33   Pinker 1999, p. 21.

6   Semantic Holism, Historicism
and Linguistic Idealism

So much for my claim that it is as hard to make the brain relevant to culture as to make hardware relevant to software. I shall end by commenting on the importance of the historicism common to Descombes, Brandom and other proponents of »linguistic idealism« – Fodor's name for the philosophical view that lies at the bottom of the slippery slope down which semantic holists descend.

Descombes' thesis that »mental vocabulary is deeply historical, which is another way of saying that there are historical conditions of meaning« parallels Brandom's view that the content of concepts becomes explicit in the course of history – in the Hegelian way in which the bud becomes explicit in the flower, and the flower in the fruit. Semantic holism tells us that meaning, or content, changes when inferential relations do. History tells us that, at least in the case of the most interesting concepts, these relations have changed a lot in recent times. Brandom thinks Hegel right in treating concepts – that is to say, uses of words – as quasi-persons, capable of maturation.

Representationalists like Fodor and Chomsky see semantic holism as causing its proponents to lose touch with reality. Since both men are subject to what Descombes calls »the general illusion of metaphysics«, they think that the world holds constant and human beings come to represent it better and better by having fewer representations of unreal things and more representations of real things. So they become impatient when they find Descombes saying »The world that must be known in order to know what the subject thinks is not just a natural world.« This is because the transactions between organism and environment that cognitive scientists study are with the environment as described in terms whose uses have not changed much in the course of history – words like »brown«, »cow«, »and«, »with,« »red«, and »yellow«. They are interested in what our children share with chimpanzees rather than in what they share with Plato.[34]

34 Consider Pinker's suggestion that »When Hamlet says ›What a piece of work is man‹ ... we should direct our attention not at Shakespeare or Mozart or Einstein or Kareem Abdul-Jabbar, but at a four-year-old carrying out a request to put a toy on a

From the point of view of linguistic idealism, nature is what, if you imagine a chimpanzee having beliefs and putting them into words, she would be
talking about. Culture is the ensemble of topics about which we doubt that
chimpanzees have any views. To put the point in another, equally rough, way:
nature is what is described by words whose use has not changed much in the
course of history and culture is what is described by those whose use has
changed quite a lot – a difference of degree, to be sure, but nevertheless an
important one. Plato, resurrected for purposes of a trans-generational collo-
quy, could quickly learn that »and« means *kai* and that »cow« means *bous*, but
it would him a lot longer to understand why »atom« does not mean *atomon*
and why neither »city« nor »nation« nor »state« means *polis*.

7 CONCLUSION

I have been arguing that one would prefer representationalism to infe-
rentialism, meaning realism to linguistic idealism, or Carnap to Wittgenstein,
only if one were subject to what Descombes calls the »general illusion of metaphysics«. For then one will think that there is a vocabulary that describes the
way things really are, and that attributing truth to our beliefs means claiming
that there is an isomorphism between the way mental representations are laid
out and the way things really are laid out. Those whom Fodor calls »linguistic
idealists« urge that we abandon the search for such an isomorphism.

Splitting the field of application of the term ›mind‹ between those who
wish to adopt what Chomsky calls »the standard methods of the natural
sciences« and those who do not, might advance the argument a little. For there
is an obvious sense in which the mind is the brain and an obvious sense in
which it is nothing of the kind, just as there is an obvious sense in which the
brain is a mass of whirling unobservable particles and another sense in which
it is not. What is needed, on the Wittgensteinian view for which I have been
arguing, is neither reduction nor synthesis, but only disambiguation.

If we could see the unity of knowledge as the ability of people using different vocabularies to stay out of each other's way, rather than as the ability to

shelf« (Pinker 1999, p. 4).

see their activities in a single synoptic vision, we would no longer be tempted by the general illusion of metaphysics. That illusion, like the idea idea, was generated by the desire for such a vision. But if we adopt Descombes' suggestion that we restrict ourselves to partial ontologies, and if we follow up on Brandom's claim that »entity« and »identity« are sortal notions, this desire would weaken. Then we will replace questions about the place of intentionality in a world of particles with questions about the place of natural science in culture. Philosophy will be not so much a matter of finding out how various things fit together as of suggesting how various social practices can coexist peaceably.

APPENDIX: PHILOSOPHY-ENVY *

When philosophers like Ortega say that we humans have a history rather than a nature they are not suggesting that we are blank slates. They do not doubt that biologists will eventually pin down the genetic factor in autism, homosexuality, perfect pitch, lightning calculation, and many other traits and abilities that differentiate some humans from others. Nor do they doubt that, back in the days when our species was evolving its way into existence on the African savannahs, certain genes were weeded out and others preserved. They can cheerfully agree with Pinker that the latter genes account for various sorts of behavior common to all human beings, regardless of acculturation.

What these philosophers doubt is that either factoring out the role of genes in making us different from one another, or tracing what we have in common back to the evolutionary needs of our ancestors, will give us anything appropriately labeled »a theory of human nature«. For such theories are supposed to be normative – to provide guidance. They should tell us what to do with ourselves. They should explain why some lives are better for human beings than other lives, and why some societies are superior to others. A theory of human nature should tell us what sort of people we ought to become.

Philosophical and religious theories of human nature flourished because they stayed clear of empirical details. They took no chances of being disconfirmed by events. Plato's and Aristotle's theories about the parts of the soul were of this sort, and so were Christianity's theory that we are all children of a loving God, Kant's theory that we are phenomenal creatures under noumenal command, and Hobbes' and Freud's naturalizing stories about the origins of sociality and of morality. Despite their lack of predictive power and empirical disconfirmability, such theories were very useful – not because they were accurate accounts of what human beings, deep down, really and truly are, but because they suggested perils to avoid and ideals to serve. They marketed helpful moral and political advice in fancy, disposable, packaging.

*   First published in *Daedalus* 133 (No. 4), 2004, pp. 18-24.

Pinker is trying to recycle this packaging, wrapping it around a miscellany of empirical facts rather than around a vision of the good life or of the good society. But it is hard to see how a composite, or a synthesis, of the various empirical disciplines that now call themselves »cognitive sciences« could serve the purposes that religions and philosophy once served. The claim that what the philosophers did a priori and badly can now be done a posteriori and well by cognitive scientists will remain empty rhetoric until its adherents are willing to stick their necks out. To make good on the promise of the term »a scientific theory of human nature« they would have to start offering advice about how we might become, individually or collectively, better people. Then they would have to spell out the inferences that had led them from particular empirical discoveries about our genes or our brains to these particular practical recommendations.

E. O. Wilson, Pinker and others who think that biology and cognitive science can take over at least part of the cultural role of philosophy are reluctant to start down this path. They remember the fate of the eugenics movement – of claims to have »proved scientifically« that interracial marriage, or increased immigration, would produce cultural degeneration. Recalling these obnoxious predecessors makes them leery of betting the prestige of their disciplines on the outcome of practical recommendations. Instead, they just repeat over and over again that as we learn more and more about our genes and our brains, we shall gain a better understanding of what we essentially are.

But for historicist philosophers like Ortega there is nothing we essentially are. There are many lessons to be learned from history, but no super-lesson to be learned from science, or religion, or philosophy. The unfortunate idea that philosophy could detect the difference between nature and convention – between what is essential to being a human being and what is merely a product of historical circumstance – was passed on from Greek philosophy to the Enlightenment. There it reappeared, in a version that would have disgusted Plato, in Rousseau. But in the last two centuries the notion that beneath all cultural overlays there lurks something called »human nature«, and that knowledge of this thing will provide valuable moral or political guidance, has fallen into deserved disrepute.

Dewey was right to mock Plato's and Aristotle's claims that the contemplative life was the one that best utilized our distinctively human abilities.

Such claims, he said, were merely ways in which these philosophers patted themselves on the back. Ever since Herder, the Rousseauvian claim that the aim of socio-political change should be to bring us back to uncorrupted nature has been rejected by thinkers impressed by the extent, and the value, of cultural variation. The idea, shared by Plato and Rousseau, that there is such a thing as the good life for man – has gradually been replaced by the conviction that there are many equally valuable human lives. This change has resulted in our present conviction that the best socio-political setup is one in which individuals are free to live whichever of these lives they choose – to make themselves up as they go along, without asking what they were somehow »meant« to become. It has also resulted in religion and philosophy being nudged aside by history, literature, and the arts as sources of edification and of ideals.

Carl Degler's »The Search for Human Nature: The Decline and Rivival of Darwinism in American Social Thought« tells the story of the biologists' attempts to move onto some of the turf from which the philosophers have been withdrawing. Darwinism revealed previously unsuspected continuities between humans and brutes, and these made it seem plausible that further biological research could tell us something morally significant. In a chapter called »Why did culture triumph?« Degler explains how the overweening pretensions of the eugenicists, and the futile attempt to stem the tide of feminism by appeals to biological facts about the differing »natures« of men and women, helped to discredit this suggestion. Then, in a chapter called »Biology redivivus«, he describes how sociobiologists and their allies have been trying to push the pendulum back in the other direction.

Degler ends his book on an ecumenical note, endorsing what Pinker calls »holistic interactionism«. But many of his readers will conclude that the moral of the story he tells is that »Nature or nurture?« was never a very good question. Darwin did make a tremendous difference to the way we think about ourselves, because he discredited religious and philosophical accounts of a gap between the truly human and immaterial part of us and the merely animal and material part. But nothing Darwin taught us blurs the distinction between what we can learn from the results of biological and psychological experiments and what we can only learn from history – the record of past intellectual and social experiments.

Pinker is right that the »nature vs. nurture« debate will not go away as long as the question is raised in respect to some very particular type of human behavior – autism, for example. But at more abstract levels, such debates are vacuous. They are rhetorical exchanges occasioned by academic turf wars. The question »Is our humanity a biological or a cultural matter?« is as sterile as »Are our actions determined or do we have free will?« No concrete result in genetics, or physics, or any other empirical discipline will help us answer either bad question. We will go right on deliberating about what to do, and holding each other responsible for actions, even if we become convinced that every thought we have, and every move we make, will have been predicted by an omniscient neurologist. We will go right on experimenting with new life-styles, new ideas, and new social institutions, even if we become convinced that, deep down, everything somehow depends on our genetic makeup. Discussion of the nature-nurture question, like discussion of the problem of free will, has no pragmatic import.

Pinker says, correctly, that there is a »widespread desire to see the whole [nature vs. nurture] issue go away« and an equally widespread suspicion that to refute a belief in the blank slate is »to tip over a straw man«. Readers of Degler will be disposed to share both that desire and that suspicion. Pinker hopes to change their minds by tipping over other straw men: »postmodernism and social constructionism, which dominate many of the humanities«. But it is hard to think of any humanist – even the most far-out Foucauldian – who would endorse the view, implausibly attributed by Pinker to Louis Menand, that »biology can provide no insight into human mind and behavior«. What Foucault, Menand, and Ortega doubt is that insights provided by biology will ever help us decide which individual and social ideals to strive for.

Pinker thinks that science may succeed where philosophy has failed. To make his case, however, he has to treat platitudes as gee-whiz scientific discoveries. He says, for example, that »cognitive science has shown that there must be complex innate mechanisms for learning and culture to be possible«. Who ever doubted there were? We already knew, before cognitive science came along, that you cannot teach young non-human animals to do things that you can teach young humans to do. We figured out a long time ago that if an organism had one kind of brain we could teach it to talk, and that if it had another kind we could not. Yet Pinker writes as if people like Menand were committed to denying evident facts such as these.

Again, Pinker cites recent suggestions that the circle of organisms that are objects of our moral concern »may be expanded by networks of reciprocal trade and interdependence and ... contracted by witnessing others in degrading circumstances«. But we did not need recent scientific research to tell us about these »possible levers of humane social change«. The relevance of interdependence to the way we treat foreign traders, and of degradation to the way we treat prisoners of war, is hardly news. People have been recommending trade and intermarriage as a way of achieving wider community for a long time now. For an equally long time, they have been suggesting that we stop degrading people in order to have an excuse for oppressing them. But Pinker describes facts familiar to Homer and Herodotus as exhibiting »nonobvious« aspects of human nature«.

It is likely that further discoveries about how our brains work will give us a lot of useful ideas about how to change human behavior. But suppose that nanotechnology eventually enables us to trace the transmission of electrical charges from axon to axon within the living brain, and to correlate such processes with minute variations in behavior. Suppose that we become able to modify a person's behavioral dispositions, in pretty much any way we like, just by tweaking her brain cells. How will this ability help us figure out what sort of behavior to encourage and what sort to discourage – to know how human beings should live? Yet that sort of help is just what philosophical theories of human nature claimed to provide.

Pinker says at various places in *The Blank Slate* that everybody has and needs a theory of human nature, and that empirical scientific inquiry is likely to give us a better theory than either uninformed common sense or a priori philosophizing. But it is not clear that we have or need anything or the sort. Every human being does have convictions about what matters more and what matters less, and thus about what counts as a good human life. But such convictions need not – and should not – take the form of a theory of human nature, or a theory of anything else. Our convictions about what really matters are constantly modified by new experiences – moving from a village to a city or from one country to another, meeting new people, and reading new books.

The idea that we deduce them, or should deduce them, from a theory is a Platonist fantasy that the West has gradually outgrown.

The books that change our moral and political convictions include sacred scriptures, philosophical treatises, intellectual and socio-political histories, epic poems, novels, political manifestoes, and writings of many other sorts. But scientific treatises have become increasingly irrelevant to this process of change. This is because, ever since Galileo, natural science has won its autonomy and its richly deserved prestige by telling us how things work, rather than, as Aristotle hoped to do, telling us about their intrinsic natures.

Post-Galilean science does not tell us what is really real or really important. It has no metaphysical or moral implications. Instead, it enables us to do things that we had not previously been able to do. When it became empirical and experimental, it lost both its metaphysical pretensions and the ability to set new ends for human beings to strive for. It gained the ability to provide new means. Most scientists are content with this trade-off. But every so often a scientist like Pinker tries to have it both ways, and to suggest that science can provide empirical evidence to show that some ends are preferable to others.

Whereas physics-envy is a neurosis found among those whose disciplines are accused of being »soft,« philosophy-envy is found among those who pride themselves on the »hardness« of their disciplines. They think that their superior rigor qualifies them to take over the roles previously played by philosophers and other sorts of humanists – roles such as critic of culture, moral guide, guardian of rationality, and prophet of the new utopia. Humanists, such scientists argue, only have opinions, but scientists have knowledge. Why not, they ask us, stop your ears against culture-babble (which is all you are going to get from those frivolous postmodernists and irresponsible social constructionists) and get your self-image from the people who know what human beings really, truly, objectively, enduringly, transculturally are?

Those who succumb to such urgings are subjected to bait-and-switch tactics. They thought that they would learn whether to be more like Antigone than like Ismene, or more like Martha than like Mary, or more like Spinoza than like Baudelaire, or more like Lenin than like FDR, or more like Ivan Karamazov than like Alyosha. They wanted to know whether they should throw themselves into campaigns for world government, or against gay marriage, or for a global minimum wage, or against the inheritance tax. They hope for the sort of guidance that idealistic freshmen still think their teachers may be able to provide. When they talk courses in cognitive science, however, this is not what they get. They get a better understanding of how their brains work, but no help in figuring out what sort of people to be or what causes to fight for.

This sense that they have been subjected to bait-and-switch tactics often afflicts freshmen who sign up for philosophy courses because they have been turned on by Marx, Camus, Kierkegaard, Nietzsche, or Heidegger. They imagine that if they take a course in what are advertised as »the core areas of philosophy« – metaphysics and epistemology – they will be better able to answer the questions these authors raised. But what they get in such courses is, typically, a discussion of the place of such things as knowledge, meaning, and value in a world made up of elementary particles. Many would-be students of philosophy are unable to see why they need have views on that topic – why they need a metaphysics.

It was because Ortega found such topics profitless that he wrote polemical essays like the one from which Pinker quotes (»History as a system«, in Ortega's *Toward a philosophy of history*). There he said

> ... all the naturalist studies on man's body and soul put together have not been of the slightest use in throwing light on any of our most strictly human feelings, on what each individual calls his own life, that life which, intermingling with others, forms societies, that in their turn, persisting, make up human destiny. The prodigious achievement of natural science in the direction of the knowledge of things contrasts brutally with the collapse of this same natural science when faced with the strictly human element (Ortega y Gasset 1941, pp. 184-185).

Ortega insisted that increasing knowledge of how things such as the human brain and the human genome work will never help us figure out to envisage ourselves and what to do with ourselves. Pinker thinks that he was wrong. But only a few pages of *The Blank Slate* grapple directly with this issue. Among those that do, the most salient are the ones in which Pinker argues that scientific discoveries give us reason to adopt what he calls »The Tragic Vision« rather than »The Utopian Vision« of human life – to take a dim view of the capacity of human beings to change themselves into new and better sorts of people.

In order to show that our choice between these two visions should be made by reference to science rather than to history, Pinker has to claim, cryptically, that »parts of these visions« consist of »general claims about how the mind works«. (p. 294) But that is just what historicist philosophers like Ortega doubt. They think that the contest between these two visions will be unaffected even if the brain turns out to work in some weird way that contemporary science has not yet envisaged, or if new fossil evidence shows that the current story about the evolution of our species is all wrong. Debates about what to do with ourselves, they say, swing as free from disagreements about the nature of neurons or about where we came as they do from controversies about the nature of quarks, or about the timing of the Big Bang.

The issue Pinker has with Ortega, and with most philosophers outside the so-called »analytic« tradition, has nothing to do with blank slates. It is about whether the conversations among humanists about alternative self-images and alternative ideals would be improved if the participants knew more about what is going on in biology and cognitive science. Pinker argues that men and women with moral and political concerns have always relied upon theories of human nature, and that empirically-based theories are now available. But Ortega would reply that for the last few hundred years we have learned to substitute historical narrative and utopian speculation for such theories.

This historicist turn owes a great deal to Darwin, the man who helped us stop thinking of ourselves as an animal body in which something extra, and specifically human, had been inserted – a mysterious ingredient whose nature poses philosophical problems. His critics said that he had reduced us to the level of the beasts, but in fact the effect of his work was to let us see imaginative daring as a causal force comparable to genetic mutation, and to think of cultural evolution as as capable of creating something radically new as is biological evolution. He helped poets like Tennyson and Whitman, and thinkers like Nietzsche, H. G. Wells, George Bernard Shaw, and John Dewey, to dream of utopias in which human beings had become as wonderfully different from us as we are from the Neanderthals. The dreams of socialists, feminists and others have produced profound changes in Western social life, and may lead to vast changes in the life of the species as a whole. Nothing that natural science tells us should discourage us from dreaming further dreams.

REFERENCES

Brandom, Robert 1994. *Making It Explicit. Reasoning, Representing and Discursive Commitment*, Cambridge, Mass.: Harvard Univ. Pr.

Chomsky, Noam 2000. *New Horizons in the Study of Language and Mind*, Cambridge: Cambridge Univ. Pr.

Crews, Frederick 2001. *Postmodern Pooh*, New York: North Point Pr.

Davidson, Donald 1986. »A nice derangement of epitaphs«, in: *Truth and Interpretation. Perspectives on the Philosophy of Donald Davidson*, ed. by Ernest Lepore, Oxford: Blackwell, pp. 433-446.

Descombes, Vincent 2001. *The Mind's Provisions. A Critique of Cognitivism*, Princeton: Princeton Univ. Pr.

Fodor, Jerry Alan 1989. *Psychosemantics. The Problem of Meaning in the Philosophy of Mind*, Cambridge, Mass.: MIT Pr.

Fodor, Jerry Alan 1994. »Why meaning (probably) isn't conceptual role«, in: *Mental Representations*, ed. by Stephen P. Stich and Ted A. Warfield, Oxford: Blackwell, pp. 142-156.

Fodor, Jerry Alan 2000a. »A science of Tuesdays«, in: *London Review of Books* 22 (No. 14, 20 July), pp. 20-21 (www.lrb.co.uk/v22/n14/fodo01_.html).

Fodor, Jerry Alan 2000b. »It's all in the mind«, in: *Times Literary Supplement* (No. 5073, 23 June), pp. 3-4.

Fodor, Jerry Alan 2002. *The Compositionality Papers*, Oxford: Clarendon Pr.

Ortega y Gasset, Jose 1941. *Toward a Philosophy of History*, New York: Norton, 1941, reprinted Urbana: Univ. of Illinois Pr., 2002.

Pinker, Steven 1999. *How the Mind Works*, New York: Norton.

Wittgenstein, Ludwig 1958. *Philosophical Investigations*, tr. by Gertrude Elisabeth Margaret Anscombe, Oxford: Blackwell.

STRONG POETS, PRIVILEGED SELF-NARRATION, AND WE LIBERALS

Three questions concerning Rorty's concept of authorship

Tim Henning, Eva-Maria Parthe, Thilo Rissing,
Judith Sieverding, and Mario Wenning

ABSTRACT: This article puts forward the following claims concerning Richard Rorty's conception of narrative self-creation: The model of the ›strong poet‹ as a reference point for Rorty's concept of individual authorship gets into conflict with his incorporation of hermeneutics as an important source of his philosophy. Rorty's concept of self-authorship ignores the influence of material and economic conditions as revealed by critical theory. Thereby it leads to a misconception of ourselves that perpetuates inequality and suffering instead of overcoming them. Rorty needs to specify who he refers to as ›we liberals‹. Moreover it is not clear how solidarity is possible, given fundamental disagreements about which collective narratives should be adopted.

KEYWORDS: hermeneutics, dialogue, strong poet, critical theory, narrative identity, authorship, liberalism, solidarity

One of the core elements of Richard Rorty's philosophy is his conception of individual and collective authorship, which he understands as a form of narrative self-creation. He defends a postmetaphysical account of history, culture and society, according to which personal, cultural or political identities do not belong to the natural equipment of the world, but are artificially created by means of storytelling. This leads him to the vision of a liberal community, which constitutes its common identity through a process of inventing collective narratives and in which everybody is free to make herself the protagonist of her individual story. This crucial point leaves a number of questions open:

(1) How can Rorty make his incorporation of hermeneutics compatible with his concept of individual authorship that is illustrated by the ›strong

poet‹?

(2) Does Rorty's concept of self-authorship ignore the influence of material and economic conditions and thereby lead to a misconception of ourselves that perpetuates inequality and suffering instead of overcoming them?

(3) Can Rorty specify who he refers to as ›we liberals‹? How is solidarity possible, given fundamental disagreements about what collective narratives should be adopted?

1

According to Rorty, individuality is a question of creating oneself by narrative description. This is to say that by telling a story about his or her life someone is enabled to develop a self-identity. The theory of narrating the self is based on the crucial thesis that there is neither an immanent essence of human nature that has to be found nor just one true language that has to be learned. The self is not supposed to be seen as a »formed, unified, present, self-contained substance, something capable of being seen steadily and whole« (CIS 41) that could be expressed in an appropriate way. Therefore creating one's self is not a process of discovery but of invention. There are as many different vocabularies as self-conscious individuals exist. Every process of self-invention is just »one more vocabulary, one more human project, one person's chosen metaphoric« (CIS 39). Inspired by the romantics, Rorty defends the idea that a successful self-invention is motivated by the desire for originality and genius. In Rorty's sense the paradigmatic model of the genius is Harold Bloom's ›strong poet‹. Just the poet's ability to describe oneself in a way no one else has even thought about before, the possibility of creating a »language of its own« (CIS 40), can fulfill the demand of self-*invention*.

As presented thus far, the self obtains its strength by differentiation from others. Nevertheless the individual has to draw the material for its own story from the contingent circumstances it is born and socialized in. Even if the creative self is able to extend his or her horizon, Rorty admits that no new draft of selfhood – as a non-normal discourse – »can avoid being marginal and parasitic« (CIS 41). In spite of the demand for originality the content of a person's new vocabulary relies on its natural, cultural and social environment. In addition, the process of individualization requires a sphere of linguistic intersubjectivity. Before a story can count as new and original the individual has to know and digest the old familiar vocabulary she shares – as a normal discourse – with all others.

Rorty considers that anything »from the sound of a word through the color of a leaf to the feel of a piece of skin can [...] dramatize and crystallize a human being's sense of self-identity« (CIS 37). However, his main focus of interest is linguistic self-invention. With regard to this respect, he stresses the need for communication in an *extraordinary* way. In order to develop a self-identity it is extremely important to be able *to talk* to others in and about the self-chosen vocabulary. Every self-created ›I‹ »desperately needs to *talk* to other people, needs this with the same urgency as people need to make love« (CIS 186). The idea of self-narration is closely connected with the necessity of ›talk‹, ›communication‹ and ›conversation‹. Rorty's description of individualization as an interactive and dialogical process reveals his incorporation of hermeneutics as an important source of his philosophy.

Given this hermeneutical presetting, Rorty's concept of authorship that is illustrated by Harold Bloom's ›strong poet‹ inevitably conjures up a momentous conflict. With his interpretation of the ›strong poet‹ Rorty refers to a concept that is characterized by a oedipal and basically not peaceable relationship between the poet and her ancestors.

Rorty claims that the ›strong poet‹ has to realize »that at a certain point one has to *trust* to the *good will* of those who will live other lives« (CIS 41). In this sense the good will of other people – out there in the future (cf. CIS 41) – is nothing else but the willingness to talk about and to take over a new vocabulary.

But – vice versa – how does the ›strong poet‹ deal with all the others and their vocabularies to which she has become acquainted in the past? The ›strong poet‹ does not seem to be on such friendly terms with her past as with her future. Bloom's poet fears nothing more than *not* being original. In order to achieve the aim of originality the ›strong poet‹ needs to overpower the others who represent the already known vocabularies: »The hope of such a poet is that what the past tried to do to her she will succeed in doing to the past: to make the past itself [...] *bear* her impress« (CIS 29).

Rorty's and »Bloom's ›horror of finding oneself to be only a copy or re-plica‹« (CIS 29) seems to deny the possibility of a real dialogical relationship between a self and others. At a certain point the ›strong poet‹ cannot esteem her predecessors as dialogue partners anymore without giving away her de-mand for originality. At a certain point she has to refuse a further conversati-on. In relation to Rorty's shining example of the ›strong poet‹ it becomes clear that the other vocabularies have to be overcome by redescription. But – in Rorty's own words – redescription often humiliates and humiliation is the worst form of cruelty (cf. CIS 90).

In his enthusiasm for the creative self-narration which is motivated by his admiration of the great exceptional individuals Rorty takes risk to instru-mentalize not only the dialogue partners but also the dialogical processes as such. He gets into conflict with his hermeneutical presetting, namely concer-ning two central aspects:

(a)   The mentioned overpowering is possible only if the dialogue partners are reduced to a *background function* as a familiar collective vocabulary the in-dividual needs as a pool for the development of its new metaphoric self-description.

(b)   The individual maintains a dialogue only until she is sure enough about her own vocabulary, that means, until she is strong enough to overpower the other vocabularies in a nearly violent way.

Dialogical processes not always have to be aimed at a consensus in the sense of an ideal conclusion. Nevertheless, the ›Horizontverschmelzung‹ that is in-tended by hermeneutics requires that dialogue partners are on the same level concerning their right to express themselves at any time. This very condition actually seems to be set aside whenever the ›strong poet‹ solely decides to break off the process of communication.

We have the suspicion that – at the end of the day – Rorty does not deal with a dialogical, but with a monological self. We would like to know how Rorty can make the very dialogical character of his philosophy compatible with his concept of »giving birth to oneself« (CIS 29) that is illustrated by the model of the ›strong poet‹.

2

According to Paul Ricoeur, there are two basic theoretical approaches towards those narratives by which we coordinate our actions, create meaning
and establish personal and cultural identities in the physical world: (1) ›Hermeneutics of suspicion‹ is based on the motivation to unmask the deceptive
character of these cultural structures. (2) The alternative approach of ›hermeneutics of trust‹ rather stresses the positive aspects of cultural achieve-
ments as conditions of possibility of human experience and practice.

In *Achieving Our Country*, Richard Rorty clearly favors the latter option,
and especially rejects the so-called *critique of ideology*. Presumably, Rorty's objection to this notion of ›ideology‹ is that it is either trivial or – if taken in a
stronger sense – even harmful: From Rorty's pragmatist point of view, the basic idea that language, meaning and self-concepts are necessarily rooted in social practices is no ›big deal‹. Accordingly, in his recent writings Rorty makes
use of a concept of ideology in a ›weak‹, non-pejorative manner. But if ›suspicion‹ is pushed to an extreme concept of ›universal power‹ (Foucault), then all
perspectives for improvement and innovation are wrecked, and this leads the
Left to fatalism. Instead of this, Rorty pleads for regaining the positive virtues
of common ›pictures and stories‹ as powerful sources of moral identity and
solidarity.

Although we agree to a large extent, certain objections concerning Rorty's complete rejection of critical theory remain. To us, there seems to be
some use in the overall idea of a critique of ideology, which could basically be
regarded as the attempt to correlate our self-descriptions with the antagonistic
social and economical forces beneath them. What Rorty's picture of a community of self-narrators does not consider sufficiently is that the practical
contexts of ›language-games‹, in which we exchange words and articulate our
concerns, are not democratic by themselves, but can easily become distorted
by underlying mechanisms of the social macrostructure.

We therefore think that certain objections put forth by critical theory are
valid – and that they are indeed a necessary addition to Rorty's point of view.
We will consider two of them:

(a) A critical claim that has been made by Richard Shusterman is that Rorty's theory of self-creation inscribes the predominant ideas of economical liberalism into the individual, thereby adapting it to external economical and social expectations. The archetype of this narrative ›autopoiesis‹ seems to be the ›flexible‹ (Sennett) individual, coping with all kinds of contingencies and innovatively responding to market tendencies – a type that in recent German politics has come to be known as the ›Ich-AG‹ (Ego Ltd. or Ego stock-corporation). But this reproach could be met with the pragmatic reply that Rorty's theory undoubtedly describes us in exactly the kind of fashion that is suitable for economic liberalism – but that this is not necessarily to be considered wrong. We doubt that this is Rorty's intention.

(b) Yet another objection might show that Rorty's theory of self-narration is in danger of falling short of its own moral ideal which is a liberal culture that encourages everyone to mark his own position within his community by modifying the common vocabulary in an authentic and unique way. But this ideal of articulating one's self in a new language, demonstrated by the ›league of extraordinary gentlemen‹ Rorty calls ›strong poets‹, is such a high aim that it can hardly be fulfilled by the majority. In spite of what Rorty and Rieff call Freud's ›democratization of genius‹, there still remains a certain *elitist* edge to the notion of a ›strong poet‹. So this ideal, originally conceived as stimulating, might reveal itself as a source of frustration as soon as it is treated as a universal standard. In addition, the overtaxed individual might be lead to indifference and the role of the mere spectator. Heroic self-creation then would turn out to be an outstanding spectacle for the ordinary mass.

To put it short: Rorty's ideal of narrative self-creation seems to generalize a highly particular social and economical situation – namely *his own*. In fact, his ideal seems to be accessible only to a few rather privileged individuals. Even if *everybody* has some creative potentials deep within his unconsciousness, it seems to be an underestimation of the complexity of the social sphere to ignore the fact that it also takes considerable amounts of *leisure* and *financial* as well as *symbolic capital* to make up an authentic identity by narration. After all, it might be that the quest for unique ways of self-articulation is not among the prior problems an average construction worker has to cope with.

Of course, this is *not* to say that moral philosophy and cultural theory are obliged to devote their concepts and arguments solely to the interests of underprivileged people. But it is a good example for the fact that the forces, interests and mechanisms inert in the social sphere can make us adopt a misleading picture of who we are and what we do – a misconception of ourselves that perpetuates inequality and suffering instead of overcoming them. This is the central reservation at the core of critical theory, whose aims we intend to defend.

3

Rorty situates himself within a tradition of inspirational liberal pragmatism with a strong sense for solidarity. We would like to raise a number of open questions, mainly with regard to what we consider to be Rorty's problematic appeal to ›us liberals‹.

Already in *Contingency, Irony and Solidarity*, Rorty links his romanticizing ethics of self-invention to his vision of society, when he sums up his argument: »the citizens of my liberal utopia would be people who had a sense of the contingency of their language of moral deliberation, and thus of their consciences and thus of their community« (CIS 61). In the subsequent *Achieving Our Country*, Rorty's appeal to a collective ›we‹ can be read as an attempt to performatively redeem his emphatically expressed need for an inspirational rhetoric. It is through taking pride in one's country, Rorty argues, that we can achieve its democratic and egalitarian potentials. Our culture of »national self-mockery and self-disgust« (AOC 8) has too long diverted our energies from enlisting solidarity to ameliorate the human condition. Rorty is well aware and sensitive to the danger of lapsing into forms of nationalism and chauvinism. This is easily lost in the tendentious translation of his book as ›Stolz auf unser Land‹. Therefore, one would miss his point, when contesting him on this issue. However, it seems fair to say that Rorty doesn't fully acknowledge the other flip side of his rhetoric of national pride, namely that it easily turns into an empty sentimental band wagoning. As Dick Bernstein puts it, »inspirational liberalism without detailed, concrete plans for action tends to become empty, just as quick fixes without overall vision and careful theoretical reflection tend to become blind« (Bernstein 2003 137).

If one wants to read Rorty against the grain, i. e. if one wants to measure him according to his own pragmatic theory of political action, one has to answer the following questions. What kind of audience is Rorty directing his proposal to, i. e. who does he expect to bring about the change to a better future? This question is bound up with the question who the ›we liberals‹ Rorty repeatedly alludes to are intended to be. Who should put his philosophy of social hope into political practice? Obviously, the political actors cannot be the self-obsessed left intellectuals Rorty is criticizing.

In drawing on romantic notions of narrative world disclosure, for example through stories about exemplary heroes, Rorty has taken steps to indicate how he envisions a transformation of public discourse. Yet, given Rorty's liberalism, it seems that everyone should have the same right to choose what heroes she wants to regard as exemplary. However desirable the goal of solidarity might be, Rorty's appeal to a canon of heroic figures hardly squares with his self-proclaimed liberalism. Certainly, Rorty cannot rely on history to defend his claim that, for specific political purposes, Dewey is more important than Helmut Kohl or Martin Luther King more so than Malcolm X. It is unclear how we are supposed to arrive at a collective ›we‹ rather than a multitude of individual voices. Rorty must be appealing to a future consensus, for the substantive values he emphatically refers to throughout his text, e. g. atheism and a plea for the primacy of change as opposed to sustainability of traditions, are far from being agreed upon even by ›us liberals‹. This is shown by the fundamental disagreement between liberal communitarians, political liberalists and libertarians. There is a tension between Rorty's espousal for growing diversity and recognition of mutual contingencies and his expressed commitment to solidarity.

Reading Rorty, it often seems as if we had a good grasp of what it means to be liberal. Yet, as Raymond Geuss has argued convincingly, liberalism is no homogeneous block, but a rough umbrella concept under which highly contested struggles about conflicting and even incompatible ›key terms‹ are being fought out (cf. Geuss 2001). Even if we drop the hope for any final vocabulary and universal standard, what kind of criteria does the political philosopher

Rorty suggest to adjudicate between conflicting traditions of – presumably bad and good – liberalism? What kind of liberal politics serves best to diminish cruelty and how can we make it compelling? Certainly Rorty cannot rest content with acknowledging that agreement is where you find it without giving up his commitment to transformative social criticism for the sake of a better future. Given these open questions it seems that Rorty needs to specify what his ›liberal utopia‹ amounts to and how we can get there.

To sum up, we have tried to show that Rorty simplifies the relationship between individual and collective types of authorship and does not pay enough attention to the complexity of and the tension within contemporary societies. Therefore he ignores certain aspects of identity formation and social structures, especially the progressive force of dialogical interaction, the emancipatory potential of critical ›hermeneutic of suspicion‹ and the various and often mutually exclusive forms of liberalism. It would be desirable if Rorty reconsidered his position with regard to these issues.

REFERENCES

Bernstein, Richard J. 2003. »Rorty's Inspirational Liberalism«, in: *Richard Rorty*, ed. by Charles Guignon and David R. Hiley, Cambridge, MA: Cambridge Univ. Pr., p. 124-138.

Geuss, Raymond 2001. *History and Illusion in Politics*, Cambridge, MA: Cambridge Univ. Pr.

THE LIBERAL IRONIST BETWEEN NATIONAL PRIDE AND GLOBAL SOLIDARITY

*Simon Derpmann, Georg M. Kleemann, Andreas Kösters,
Sebastian Laukötter, and David Schweikard*

ABSTRACT: This essay deals with two aspects of Rorty's political philosophy: Rorty's plea for the return to the nation-state as the only political agent which is capable of realizing the liberal hope on the one hand, and the concept of national pride as the main focus of political identification and motivation on the other. It develops critical notes by pointing at the limits of the nation state as a political agent and national pride as its basis. As an alternative to Rorty's conception of national pride it presents an extensive conception of solidarity.

KEYWORDS: solidarity, national pride, irony, reformist and cultural left

INTRODUCTION

Utopias, metaphors and stories are rarely referenced in political articulation. Although describing a state of social or political perfection, they are considered impractical for actual political development. To Richard Rorty, *exactly these* forms of articulation are needed for political progress. He thinks that through a competition of ideas of this kind, »a state of less unnecessary suffering« and »the creation of greater diversity of individuals« (AOC 30) might be achieved. Rather than questioning whether a fruitful political practice can evolve from the use of utopias, metaphors or stories, we seek to evaluate *which* utopias, metaphors and stories should be promoted.

Rorty's political suggestions, as prominently expressed in his book *Achieving Our Country*, strive to show how to regain the capacity of political action in socially and politically influential global structures. In comparison with the somewhat successful »reformist Left«, the current »cultural Left« seems to him »unable to engage in national politics. It is not the sort of Left which can be asked to deal with the consequences of globalization.« (AOC 91.) In order to abandon the role of mere spectatorship in favour of accurate political activism, Rorty proposes to cultural leftists not only to »put a moratorium on theory« but also »to mobilize [...] [their] pride in being Americans« (AOC 91).

Rorty's concept of national pride corresponds to his idea of solidarity as the main basis of political action developed in *Contingency, Irony and Solidarity*. According to Wilfrid Sellars' analysis of moral obligations as »we-intentions«, solidarity depends on the perception of someone as »one of us«, as belonging to a »we-group«. In *Achieving Our Country* it is the nation-state that is specified as the only relevant »we-group« of reference in practicing a liberal policy of social justice.

In what follows, we will deal with two aspects: the plea for the return to the nation-state as the only political agent capable of realizing the liberal hope, as well as the concept of national pride as the main focus of political identification and motivation. We will develop our critical notes by first pointing out limits of the nation-state as a political agent and national pride as its basis. Our critique concerns both the potentials for political action in a globalized world and some of Rorty's philosophical assumptions. In a second step we want to present a different, *extensive* conception of solidarity. We consider this a more plausible and at the same time – to adopt one of Rorty's notions – a more useful »utopia« for a political practice within the global order.

1   LIMITS OF THE NATION-STATE AND NATIONAL PRIDE

1.1   *Practical Problems*

Faced with the choice of coping with the challenges of globalization on either an international or national level – two conflicting strategies according to Rorty (AOC 88) – he clearly opts for the latter. According to him »the government of our nation-state will be, for the foreseeable future the only agent capable of making any real difference in the amount of selfishness and sadism inflicted on Americans.« (AOC 98.) Every attempt to promote an international solution could only be a continuation of national initiatives. (AM 984.)

This means that each country is first required to develop a national consciousness (a task that is still undone in most developing countries) before something like a cosmopolitan responsibility can evolve. (SDW 19.)

In our opinion, depicting the nation-state as a necessary condition for any further political action is not promising for two reasons. To begin with, Rorty's analysis is closely tied to an understanding of the United States as an economic, military and political superpower whose decisions on the national level can have a significant impact on the international level. But what may be valid in this special case cannot necessarily be applied to other countries. Especially the developing-countries, whose population should be regarded as the primary target group of the project »less unnecessary suffering«, would remain internationally insignificant even as consolidated nation-states.

Secondly, and more importantly, it is doubtful that under the conditions of a globalized economy even the United States still possesses the possibility to reduce social injustice within its own national borders. Rorty, himself, asserts that »Globalization is producing a world economy in which an attempt by any one country to prevent the immiseration of its workers may result only in depriving them of employement.« (AOC 85.) The economic cosmopolitans who shirk their social and national responsibilities keep up the illusion that something could still be changed:

> For they need people who can pretend to be the political class of each of the individual nation-states. For the sake of keeping the proles quiet, the super-rich will have to keep up the pretense that national politics might someday make a difference. (AOC 87 f.)

Considering this, a liberal course of political action, operating with the nation-state as its only reference and, consequently, with national pride as the prevailing form of common identity, will not be able to respond to the social, economic or ecological challenges of globalization. Accepting the present inability to act on a supranational level and restricting oneself to one's own domestic problems further empowers the initiatives of the cosmopolitan super-rich, for they will be the only profiteers of the competition between the nation-states and their social and economic policies.

1.2   Conceptual Problems

The problems we have with Rorty's conception of the nation-state and national pride partly stem from what one could call the »socioeconomic facts« of
globalization, but they also refer to the relation between some of his political
suggestions and their philosophical background. Leaving aside Rorty's remarks on the relation between politics and philosophy, his »political« book
Achieving Our Country and the »philosophical« book *Contingency, Irony and Solidarity* share a striking similarity: they both treat the problem of (moral or political) identity as the basis of the capacity to act and they both use the vocabulary of self-creation.[1] Political and moral actions are based on the identification
with a »we-group«. This »we-group« cannot be »found« in nature or in history,
but has to be constructed and confirmed in »the form of historical narration
and utopian speculation.« (CLC 60.) Rorty intends to show this in *Achieving
Our Country* as he explicitly admits:

> Nations rely on artists and intellectuals to create images of, and to tell
> stories about, the national past. Competition for political leadership is in
> part a competition between differing stories about a nation's self-identi-
> ty, and between differing symbols of its greatness. (AOC 4.)

Therefore, Bloom's »Strong Poet« is not only the paradigm for private, idio-
syncratic self-creation, but also for the collective, thus public and political,
identity. Thus Rorty does not hesitate to call the United States »the first thor-
oughgoing experiment in national self-creation« (AOC 22) and to regard it »as
both self-creating poet and self-created poem.« (AOC 29.) This corresponding use of the vocabulary of self-creation in regard to both individual and collective identity undermines Rorty's strict separation between self-creation as
the (private) sphere of the ironist and politics as the (public) sphere of the liberal. We take this to justify our problems with the fact that Rorty, in developing his project of national self-creation via national pride, ignores aspects
which play a central role in his concept of private self-creation. We will now
specify two of theses aspects.

---

1   For a more detailed analysis, cf. *Strong Poets, Privileged Self-Narration, and We Liberals* in
this volume.

Firstly, given Rorty's emphasis on novelty as the core of his notion of progress, and given the novelty of the challenges of globalization, it is difficult to understand why Rorty sticks to the old-fashioned concept of the nation-state in order to conceive a collective identity. His own project of »de-diviniz-ation« is meant »to substitute a tissue of contingent relations, a web which stretches backward and forward through past and future time, for a formed, unified, present, self-contained substance, something capable of being seen steadily and whole«. (CS 41.) Thus, individual identity is constructed as a kind of network. The nation-state, in contrast, still seems to play the role of a polit-ical equivalent of the self-contained subject, in order to be the only remaining guarantor for integrity and wholeness, the only remaining divinity. Neverthe-less Rorty himself characterizes the most powerful political movements from American history as networks and alliances of heterogeneous groups. But if we accept the idea of network-identities in the fields of politics, then it is hard to see why these networks should have to come to a halt at national borders, when the structures they work against pass through national borders freely. Thus, what is of importance is not the immediate feasibility of such institu-tions, but rather the refinement of the philosophical creativity necessary for their construction. Although Rorty regards the creative imagination of altern-atives as the essential instrument of social change,[2] in the matters of political identity and action this very concept is not fully realized.

Secondly: to Rorty, national pride is the central element of the creation of a political identity. But when he describes national pride as the belief in one's country and thus as a kind of civic religion, or when he compares the narrative constitution of the American identity to the »platoon«-movies as sources of an American team spirit, one might wonder how he wants to pre-vent national pride from turning into bellicosity and militaristic chauvinism – things he avowedly wants to avoid. In the private sphere irony can serve as a protectant from arrogance or false self-satisfaction: »The ironist spends her time worrying about the possibility that she has been initiated into the wrong tribe, taught to play the wrong language game.« (PILH 75.) The problem is

2   »Ich hätte gedacht, dass die Befreiung von bisherigen sozialen Determinanten ty-pischerweise daraus resultiert, dass jemand phantasievolle Alternativen zu bisherigen Praktiken nennt und damit zu neuen Vorschlägen für künftige Handlungen anregt« (EMF 261).

that Rorty exiles irony from the public and from the political sphere, restrict-ing it to the sphere of private idiosyncrasy. In a political context, he insinu-ates, irony tends to become an attitude of self-loathing and self-disgust; an obsession with authenticity and purity, leading to political abstinence. This results in Rorty's dismissal of the very possibility of »a culture whose public rhetoric is *ironist*.« (PILH 87, Rorty's italics.)

Yet, the virtues of the ironist seem indispensable in original political mat-ters. If it is true »that feelings of solidarity are necessarily a matter of which similarities and dissimilarities strike us as salient, and that such salience is a function of a historically contingent final vocabulary« (S 192), then an ironic attitude that permanently questions the limits of this vocabulary is just as ne-cessary on a public level as it is on the private. Otherwise, the self-doubt sur-rounding the adequacy of one's own sensitivity and present institutional ar-rangements for dealing with pain and humiliation of others (S 198) would be-come simply a private attitude unconcerned with questions of social cruelty or economic injustice.

2   Solidarity

Extended solidarity need not be affected by the doubts we have articulated. To do so, it must maintain a crucial potential of attainability. Additionally, extended solidarity must also be a possible source of useful political agents and actions. After a short sketch of the function of extended solidarity we will discuss two arguments against it.

2.1   The Function of Solidarity

Wherever the political challenges mentioned above are to be faced, global structures will have to replace smaller agents. The common aim, »less unne-cessary suffering« and a »greater diversity of individuals«, depends on new channels of political influence. This change in the political agents (institu-tions, political organizations of all kinds etc.), that are yet to come or, if they can be found already, to be strengthened, will have to be accompanied by a change in the self-understanding of their constituent individuals. Within these institutions an *extensive solidarity*, if not a global one, will have to exist rather than national pride. It will have to unite the participants of those institutions making them aware that some of their problems can only be faced by a collective and thus not individually, locally or nationally.

If solidarity exists among people, they have the feeling of belonging together and of contrast to those who are not part of their group. What connects them might be certain convictions, capabilities, habits, or a shared self-understanding. Solidarity can cause strong unification in smaller groups like families, neighborhoods and among friends. But it also appears in larger groups, where its impact may decrease, e. g. among people with the same aesthetical preferences, political aims, cultural background etc. One can be a member of several different »we-groups« at a time and thus be connected with others through solidarity in various ways and with differing aims. Some forms of solidarity are important, some hazardous, and some barely perceptible. Their weight depends upon which impacted aspects of life – such as the creation of identities or social and political practices – are being examined.

In our view Rorty's *national pride*, the emotional involvement with a country and its inhabitants, is a form of solidarity which is insufficient, even hindering, when it comes to creating institutions and bringing about action within the global order that influences more and more spheres of human life. Instead of *national pride* there is the need and – as we hope to show – the option for an extensive solidarity.

2.2   Arguments Against Extensive Solidarity

(a)   Essentialism

Rorty rejects the traditional understanding of »human solidarity« that implies the existence of something specifically and naturally human that we can relate to, if we recognize it in others. He has no use for the notion that »[...] finite, mortal, contingently existing human beings might derive the meanings of their lives from anything except other finite, mortal, contingently existing human beings.« (CLC 45.)

But the assumption that there is something all human beings share does not imply that these qualities would have to be independent of human wishes and desires. Even without arguing for the intrinsicality of certain values, one could still regard them as a plausible human capacity. Thus, although *not* ahistorical principles, they could serve for an extensive solidarity. Rorty's »liberal ironist« embodies such a kind of solidarity, since »[s]he thinks that what unites her with the rest of the species is not a common language but just susceptibility to pain and in particular to [...] humiliation.« (PILH 92.) This is different from the national pride proclaimed by Rorty in *Achieving Our Country*.

(b)   Factual Limits of Solidarity

Rorty wants humans to extend their »we-groups« as far as possible, but nevertheless he thinks that this process soon finds its limits. According to him, the »we« derives its strength from a contrast. So if the »we« extended to all humans, there would be no one to be part of the »they« and a solidarity felt universally would cease to have identificational and motivational force.

But if, as seen, stories and utopias are involved in the creation of identity, a historical or an imaginary, instead of a factual contrast should be sufficient for the distinction. Even if a factual difference were essential to Solidarity, why would it depend upon national boundaries? One could probably find strong grounds for solidarity with others independent of the arbitrary bounds of a nation. Simultaneously social differences within a country make some forms of solidarity unlikely. »He is a father just like I am« or »She is a worker just like I am« are more likely to generate solidarity than »She is an American just like I am«, because they refer to a significant quality that is actually *felt* to be shared. Rorty should agree, because solidarity according to him is »[...] the ability to see more and more traditional differences [...] as unimportant when compared with the similarities with respect to pain and humiliation.« (S 192.) Compared with these similarities and differences there is not much in a language or a country that would make it reasonable to stick to a form of solidarity that is becoming politically obsolete.

3   Can Extensive Solidarity Replace National Pride?

Which solidarity we propose will have an influence on our self-understanding and on our political practice, and eventually on the institutions that can become politically meaningful. An extensive solidarity is not a useful basis for the specific aims of a family or among friends, but when it comes to issues, of which the outcome is determined by processes that go beyond the national borders – the exact issues that are most important to Rorty in this context – it certainly is. With an extensive solidarity we could embark upon political identities and agents adequate both to the challenges of the global order and to Rorty's own philosophical background. One could stand up for »less unnecessary suffering and a greater diversity of individuals« and still see those aims as contingent, non-objective truths, ever evolving, yet dependent upon human wishes and desires and, therefore, worthy of one's exertions. It would allow a public irony to permanently question the range of such solidarity, and there would be the possibility to establish political networks which unite heterogeneous groups in order to pursue common aims.

In fact, extensive solidarity can be found quite commonly. Many people revere ideas like the *Universal Declaration of Human Rights*. They become aware of and participate in organizations against the exploitation of workers in the developing countries, for transparency and fairness in trade, for environmental protection and for medical and educational care. The success of these organizations depends upon an extensive solidarity. If individuals stood unflinchingly for their beliefs, in spite of their idiosyncrasy and contingency, Rorty's liberal ironist would encourage them to do so, because she argues that one will find no universal or eternal justification for any belief. Emotional involvement with what one does need not be directed towards a country, but rather towards something that one has more grounds to relate to. Both local and extensive solidarity should be embraced. Solidarity needs to be local to make the discovery of »ever more novel, ever richer, forms of human happiness« (AOC 30) possible, but at the same time extensive to guarantee that the foundations of these forms will not vanish.

PRAGMATISM, REALISM, AND SCIENCE

From Argument to Propaganda

*Marius Backmann, Andreas Berg-Hildebrand, Marie Kaiser, Michael Pohl,
Raja Rosenhagen, Christian Suhm, and Robert Velten*

ABSTRACT: Richard Rorty is well known as a propagandist of pragmatism and of a »post-philosophical«
culture in which many traditional philosophical debates are dismissed as outrightly fruitless. The paper
is mainly concerned with Rorty's dismissal of the realism-antirealism debate. The shift from argument
to propaganda which is typical of much of Rorty's reasoning is critically investigated from different
perspectives. In particular, it is argued that Rorty cannot convincingly establish a pragmatist position
beyond realism and antirealism, and that pragmatism seems to be inadequate with respect to scientific
practice. Finally, the fruitfulness of the realism-antirealism debate is defended.

KEYWORDS: pragmatism, realism, realism-antirealism debate, science

INTRODUCTION

Richard Rorty is known as a philosopher who does not want to be a traditional philosopher anymore. Instead of this he envisages becoming a ›post-philosophical‹ pragmatist living in a »culture without centre« (cf. KOZ), in which
no privileged or fundamental status is attributed to either philosophy or science. In order to reach this ›post-philosophical‹ culture, Rorty is eager to dismiss notorious philosophical debates and to replace them by pragmatist discourses. In particular, Rorty recommends abandoning the entire realism/an-
tirealism debate. His main reasons for this are the enduring fruitlessness of
the debate and the threat of scepticism it evokes.

Instead of adopting one of the traditional positions within the realism/antirealism debate, Rorty advocates the »Natural Ontological Attitude«[1] which was introduced into the debate on scientific realism by Arthur Fine. (Cf. Fine 1986.) This debate is centred upon the questions whether our most successful theories by the mature natural sciences deliver at least approximately true accounts of the physical world and whether there is such a thing as scientific progress by approximation to truth. Rorty answers both questions in the negative, at least so far as truth means some sort of correspondence relation between what theories say about the world and features of the world itself.

An adherent of NOA, however, refuses to get involved in a couple of, as she thinks, futile discussions on the scientifically adequate theory of truth or approximation to truth. When it comes to such metaphysical questions, a ›knower‹ (as we might call the defender of NOA according to Fine himself) or a Rortian pragmatist will remain silent or possibly express her disregard with an ironic smile.

In this paper we argue that Rorty dismisses the realism-antirealism debate too rashly. We will do this by means of investigating the impact this dismissal has on Rorty's account of the natural sciences.

In doing so, we are also concerned with Rorty's strategy to withdraw from arguments and to shift to propaganda which is typical of much of his reasoning. He often seems, nonetheless, to take part in the debate by giving special arguments, mainly directed against realism. But when faced with counterarguments he shifts to propaganda claiming that he is not willing to take part in the debate anymore, and dismisses it outright. He recommends the search for a new vocabulary which should (in a distant future) prove the absurdity of the ongoing debate. (BRA 113.) In correspondence to the steps of this strategy, we will meet Rorty on three different levels.

In the *first* part of our paper we meet Rorty on the level of argument and hope to show that Rorty's position is not at all to be located »beyond realism and antirealism« (BRA), despite his claims to the contrary, and that his overall account of the epistemological status of the natural sciences is misleading.

In the *second* part we examine several problems which Rorty's pragmatist position faces in the light of actual scientific (and social) practice. Under the

1   Cf. BRA 108 f., hereafter abbreviated as »NOA«.

heading of three questions we focus on the notion of »usefulness« and its applicability (here an excursion to the aspect of rationality is included), on the consequences Rorty's pragmatism has on scientific practice, and on the grounds scientists might have for adopting a pragmatist stance.

Finally, we try to meet Rorty on the level of propaganda and propagate – contrary to his pragmatism – the continuation of the realism/antirealism debate.

1 RORTY ON SCIENTIFIC REALISM

In order to expel the natural sciences from the centre of our culture, Rorty tries to show that natural science is not a natural kind. He thinks so on the basis that there is neither a special methodology by which natural science could be defined, nor a special relation between scientific theories and reality. According to Rorty's pragmatist likings, only the Baconian criteria of prognostic success and manipulation of nature – both decisive for technical progress – will serve for the distinction between science and non-science.[2]

Closely related to this line of arguing is Rorty's dismissal of abductive reasoning or inference to the best explanation as a genuine logical tool for science. (Cf. ibid., p. 53.) Furthermore, he distrusts the power of the so called no miracle-argument that is essential for a defense of scientific realism. (Cf. ibid., p. 54.) The success of science, the realist concludes, would be a miracle if scientific theories were not at least approximately true. Rorty, however, tries to undermine this argument by asking whether there are different ways of testing the explanandum (the success of science) and the explanans (the truth of scientific theories). In his opinion, the idea of a (nearly) true theoretical description of the world as it is in itself, i. e., independent of our theoretical commitments, loses much of its cogency, if making true predictions is all we can ask for with regard to both a theory's success and its truth. The notoriously troublesome realist's conception of the relation between theory and world should therefore evaporate into a dim remembrance of what once was of serious philosophical concern.

2   Cf. NSK 47 (»ability to predict and control«).

Two aspects of Rorty's criticism of scientific realism and his advocacy of NOA are questionable. First, there seems to be no dependence of scientific realism (or even the comprehensibility of the entire realism/antirealism debate) on the fact that science is a natural kind. Why should we dismiss the idea of science giving us a true picture of the world, since basic scientific methods, e. g., abductive reasoning, can certainly be successfully employed in non-scientific contexts of our daily life?

Second, Rorty himself cannot escape realism. He underpins his position in the philosophy of mind, which is a non-reductive physicalism, by a thoroughly realistic supposition, namely the existence of mind-independent causal relations that remain stable and constant under various descriptions. (Cf. CTT 88.) Rorty anticipates the realist's demand for answering the question whether such causal relations constitute the real and true structure of a mind-independent world, or are simply due to a pragmatic or regulative ideal we pursue in doing research. In Rorty's opinion, however, distinguishing between real and true causal relations on the one hand and ideals of research on the other, is just another case of being trapped in the dichotomy between scheme and content, i. e., the third dogma of empiricism. (Cf. Davidson 1984c, p. 189.) Moreover, he believes that Donald Davidson convincingly demonstrated that this distinction cannot be held on to and that we should generally cease to separate features of the world as it is in itself from features of the world that obtain only for us.

In our view, this response to the realist's challenge simply begs the question. If Rorty presupposes that we stand in causal relations with the world, and if he furthermore assumes that these relations remain constant under different descriptions (e. g., physical and mental descriptions), he has to face one of the two following consequences. Either he is forced to accept some sort of ontological realism, namely the thesis that at least the causal structure of the world is independent of us, hence a feature of the world in itself.[3] Or Rorty is in need of a constructivist-like account of causality according to which causal

---

3   According to Michael Devitt, ontological realism in that sense is all that is needed to deem Rorty as a realist, since there is, contrary to what Rorty claims, no further necessary relation between ontological realism on the one hand and a correspondence theory of truth on the other; cf. Devitt 1987.

relations are somehow imposed on the world by us, which would clearly amount to an antirealist position of the idealistic type.

We do not see how a mere refusal to make a choice here, resulting in the dismissal of the entire realism/antirealism debate, can be anything more than the plain confession of the lack of any argument. Rorty claims that we should rather change the philosophical vocabulary. But this, in our opinion, simply amounts to an unfair withdrawal from argument in favor of a propagandist strategy. We will turn to this strategy in part (3), but before doing this we will investigate whether Rorty's pragmatism as such can be regarded as a coherent approach.

2   PRAGMATISM AND SCIENCE

As we have seen, Rorty regards the debate between realists and antirealists as fruitless and, therefore, recommends its abandonment. (PRM 57.) Instead of continuing the debate, philosophers' attention should focus on discussions which are more useful to society and lead to practical results. There seem to be at least three interlacing problems arising from this approach.

Problem A: What is the meaning of »usefulness«?

It does not seem to be at all clear, whether we are really able to understand and evaluate what it means for a decision to be useful. Following Rorty, the concept of »being useful« surely cannot refer to something generally and necessarily true. (ITGI 41.) What is meant by the expression »useful« must at best depend on what a particular society, which commits itself to specific aims and values, can agree on. In some, if not in most cases, it will be defined by different parts of a society, or even by each individual member of it, in a quite different manner. Rorty obviously presupposes that most of his readers can agree on such aims as pluralism, liberalism, democracy, prosperity, wealth, and the prevention of suffering and humiliation, in short, a Rortian or Western perspective on a better future. Rorty apparently believes these aims to be so well established in our culture that they are not in need of any further or absolute justification.

In *Truth and Progress,* Rorty tries to capture a glimpse of what »useful« or – more generally – »better« might mean by giving the following tentative explanation: »Better« is what »will come to seem better to *us*«. (PRM 55.) This vaguely characterizes those beliefs, theories, and actions as better ones, which a society (or part of a society or an individual) considers more comfortable, more coherent, or more helpful – simply somehow better for the achievement of the respective aims. Additionally, such beliefs, theories, etc. are supposed to be more adequate in order to solve problems and to be applicable to more relevant phenomena than others. Rorty admits that the criteria he offers for evaluating them are neither necessary nor sufficient to determine what the meaning of »better« is or should be. Rather, he tries to convince us that it is not even urgent to delineate what is meant by »better« in advance, as we shall reach a sufficient agreement on the meaning of the term after a long and goal-defining discourse in society.

Nevertheless, as Rorty refuses to give us a specific criterion in advance, the use, which subsequent decisions have had, can only be properly evaluated in retrospect. But whether a decision is of any use for society, is a question which should be thoroughly considered, since what is considered useless today could turn out to be extremely useful tomorrow or vice versa.

Let us explain this by means of the natural sciences: How are we supposed to know whether a battery of particularly expensive scientific experiments will eventually lead to the development of some useful devices in an unknown future? The employment of the Baconian criteria of science (control, forecast) would expect too much from the respective experts. It is impossible to decide which activities will lead to technological improvements in the long run (as nobody could have foreseen that quantum mechanics would lead to semiconductor-technology).[4] It seems to be more useful to technological progress to accept natural sciences as a natural kind, which implies that they have their own methods by which we investigate the (mind-independent) world.[5]

---

4   The decision of how to distribute limited resources of a society could be made on the basis of Rorty's pragmatic considerations. But this should not be mixed up with the *definition* of science. It is absurd to claim that a physicist who is denied the public funding of, e. g., a very expensive particle accelerator will, in consequence, not be called a scientist any longer.

Some general remarks about the conditions which are necessary in order to find an agreement might be appropriate here. It seems to be clear that such a process as finding an agreement is crucially dependent on the ability to understand what it is that the respective opponent is trying to say. Donald Davidson and others have argued that we have to apply the principle of charity in order to enable ourselves to understand what a speaker of a (foreign) language says and intends.[6] Davidson claims that »as we must maximize agreement, or risk not making sense of what the alien is talking about, so we must maximize the self-consistency we attribute to him, on pain of not understanding *him*«. (Davidson 1984a, p. 27.) If we are somehow not able to »interpret the utterances and other behavior of a creature as revealing a set of beliefs largely consistent and true by our own standards, we have no reason to count that creature as rational, as having beliefs, or as saying anything«. (Davidson 1984b, p. 137.) Rorty, although he generally refers to Davidson in a very approving way, can probably not agree with him here, as Rorty can certainly not wish to make the strong claim that the ability to understand something is necessarily linked to a specific concept of rationality that is generally true, namely the one we use. On the contrary, Rorty claims that what truth, moral standards, standards of rationality, logical laws and the like are depends on the conventions which a respective group of people has agreed on.[7] This dependence makes the outcome a contingent and not a necessary one, and Rorty mentions no further restrictions on the process of agreement itself. He must in consequence embrace the possibility that other standards of rationality exist and are in use, which are consistent in their own way of conceiving consistency and which involve their own ways of coming to an agreement, of

5   This does not mean that scientific realism is true, because antirealist philosophers of science would agree with this description of science but differ on the epistemological status of scientific theories.

6   See for instance Henderson 1987. Henderson argues that at least at the beginning, when the development of a translation manual is at issue, the principle of charity is crucial in order to come to a first approximation of an understanding of the foreign language. In a second step, it has to be weakened in order to avoid the problem of irrationality, i. e., to make possible in that language the expression of irrational beliefs and irrational actions which are well-documented facts in psychology and human sciences.

7   This claim can be implicitly and explicitly found throughout TP. Moreover, Rorty insisted on it in discussion.

defining and justifying the concept of being »useful«. Some will probably stop here and take this position as self-defeating, as not being at all plausible, but if it is taken seriously, it seems to be fairly ineffective and inappropriate to use our standards of rationality, when several groups with supposedly different standards each are involved. Actually it is hard to see how any understanding or any further agreement could be reached on such a basis, if the standards of rationality involved differ to a significant degree.

What are we to make of this? Rorty might try to defend his position by saying that we normally do not encounter such problems, as we all talk most of the times more or less along the same lines of logic and rationality, so that the question, whether or not the contingency of our own standards would pose a problem in discourse, is pragmatically irrelevant. But this reply can only beg the question, as it presupposes what Rorty himself cannot grant, i. e., that we all in fact do use the same general standards. So the problem of possibly different standards remains and allows the unsatisfying possibility that we actually cannot come to an agreement on what »useful« means, because we generally cannot be sure whether we are able at all to make sense of what other people are saying, as our standards of rationality simply do not apply to their reasoning.

In order to avoid this unfavorable result it seems to be a more plausible and even a more viable method from a pragmatic point of view to avoid any relativistic notions regarding the standards of rationality and the laws of logic. For it seems difficult to see how a logic which deviates significantly from our logic, i. e., one which allows one or more forms of contradictions and paradoxes, could appear and how it could be used in order to establish any satisfactory cognitive theory.[8] Of course the arguments just mentioned are not sufficient to show, that other standards of rationality and logic are impossible. They only show that it would be hard to form an empirically adequate theory which explains the fact that we usually are able to come to an agreement without referring to universal concepts of rationality.

8   For a concept of minimal rationality see Cherniak 1981. Cherniak argues that – for understanding what it is to have a belief – some minimal deductive abilities, such as the ability to form useful inferences and the ability to eliminate inconsistencies in the belief set, are indispensable.

Problem B: What exactly are the consequences of Rorty's pragmatism?

It remains at least vague as to what the exact consequences of pragmatism are, if we follow Rorty's suggestions regarding the notion of usefulness in the context of science and scientific practice. According to our interpretation, Rorty claims that there is a difference between traditional philosophy and pragmatism, especially when it comes to estimating their respective influences on the sciences as parts of a society. Rorty underscores the view that traditional philosophy does not have any, or at best a very marginal, influence on what and how scientists think and act. (SRR 76.) Thus, Rortian pragmatism does not substitute former philosophy. Rather, it introduces itself as an entirely new paradigm for the organization of a liberal society that lacks any kind of institution so central or predominant as, for example, science in contemporary Western countries.

Rorty envisages pragmatism – at least in the long run – to result in significant improvements of the social development. What this means, however, remains obscure and sketchy at best. The pragmatist scientist that Rorty has in mind can be characterized as someone who has successfully managed to forget all about the old philosophical dichotomies as well as the classical philosophical problems, and who is therefore able to contribute to a productive and useful discourse within a more liberal and pluralistic society (ibid.).

We think that there are at least three points on which a further clarification is necessary. *First*, what consequences does Rortian pragmatism have – or which should it have – for the attitudes and convictions scientists have regarding their work? *Second*, what consequences follow from the scientists' attitudes towards society in general, and towards the sciences in particular, and in what respect can pragmatist scientists be »better citizens of a better academic community«? (Ibid.) *Third*, does Rortian pragmatism result in a significant change of scientific practice, including experimental methods and the testing of hypotheses? And to what consequences does this change finally lead?

Problem C: Why should scientists and the society accept Rorty's pragmatism?

It might be worth considering whether it is utopian to assume that members of today's scientific communities would accept a pragmatist conception of natural sciences in the long run. Paradoxically, from a pragmatic perspective it seems to be much more useful to stick to a realist than to a pragmatist position. Authority, social and economical influence, and a high social status in general, which are usually attributed to scientists in modern societies, depend heavily on the assumption that scientists are, or at least pretend to be, discoverers of mind-independent features of an objective world, i. e., realists. To abandon this realist attitude, be it adopted truly or not, could end up in a breakdown of the sciences' privileged position in society and the high esteem they are held in. Clearly, this is a consequence many scientists may not be willing to accept, and more pressing for a pragmatist approach, should not accept *for pragmatic reasons.* Moreover, Rorty's idea of a culture without centre aims at a society, where the predominant status of any part of a society can be nothing more than temporary. We do not see, though, how even a society of pragmatists could come to a point where the predominant status of science would be denied. At least up to now, science has been extremely useful to society, so that, *for pragmatic reasons* again, this status is attributed to science, and there is no reason to think that this is going to change.

Apart from the problems discussed so far, we consider it to be a much more plausible assumption that philosophical debates do have a direct influence on scientists and their practices. As Rorty's fellow philosopher of science, Arthur Fine, pointed out within his reconstruction of Einstein's philosophical attitudes, at least the two fundamental revolutions in physics of the 20th century were strongly motivated by an antirealist perspective. (Fine 1986, p. 124.) If this is correct, scientific developments heavily rely on a direct connection between philosophy and science, which Rorty seems to disbelieve.

At this point, one could argue that it is a rather empirical question whether physicists or other scientists are participating in philosophical debates. It can even be argued that most of the scientists do not care about such rather obscure things like philosophy. On the other hand, Fine has, as stated above, shown quite clearly that some of the most respected scientists very well did.[9] The question arises how one can avoid reflecting on the status of scientific theories when doing research that seems to defy common theories that seem to work perfectly well. Of course, this problem is more likely to

9   It is, by the way, questionable whether Fine's NOA is plausible if his description of Einstein's and Bohr's antirealist philosophical standpoints is correct.

show up at times of so-called scientific revolutions. This would explain why most scientists do not care about the philosophy of science, as many try to maintain. Scientific revolutions have always been the work of only a handful of radical minds. It seems implausible that a person at such a high level of reflection ignores the philosophical consequences of her scientific work.

In contrast to Rorty, we think that modern physics provides a good example of how philosophical assumptions turn out to be fruitful for scientific progress. We therefore do not see why a scientist should subscribe to a pragmatic understanding of science. On the contrary, adopting a pragmatic stance would deprive him of his motivational and inspirational force which enables him to develop new ideas and methods.

In sum, as we do not see any convincing reasons for either society or scientists to accept the pragmatic view of science, the question arises as to how Rorty is able to imagine pragmatism to come into force at all.

3   COUNTERPROPAGANDA

Let us now switch to the propagandist level of discourse. Rorty could still try to sabotage our efforts by claiming that we misinterpreted his approach as a special form of antirealism, hence, unfairly attempt to force him back into a philosophical debate which he considers to be useless. Since it is the aim of Rorty's pragmatism to get rid of fruitless philosophical controversies altogether, we should, he suggests, envisage a new vocabulary completely incommensurable with the conceptual frameworks of traditional philosophy.

The problem, however, is that such a vocabulary does not yet exist. It is therefore exceedingly difficult for Rorty not to fall back into old dichotomies when he tries to advocate pragmatism. Nevertheless, he advises that we »create *causes* for forgetting old controversies, which are not *reasons* for forgetting them«. (BRA 114.) A »temporary forgetfulness« (ibid.) about old controversies might lead to the development of a new vocabulary and to a withdrawal from traditional philosophical disputes. The stress on »causes« rather than on »reasons« clearly indicates that here Rorty switches from argument to propaganda. He tries to convince us that pragmatism is a standpoint beyond realism and antirealism not only by giving arguments that are directed against one or the other, but also by propagating the abandonment of the whole debate.

By changing the level of discourse from argument to propaganda, Rorty evokes the anti-pragmatist propaganda of which we are now going to give a brief sketch. Anti-pragmatist propaganda is to be located on a meta-philosophical level beyond any traditional philosophical debate, which brings it on a par with Rorty's pragmatism. In particular, we will try to urge the continuation of the realism/antirealism debate and highlight its many advantages.

Rorty claims that philosophical debates have been long and fruitless, and especially, that there has been no significant progress in the realism/antirealism debate in the last four or five decades.[10] We consider this as a quite unfair evaluation. Beginning from logical positivism, Popper's falsificationism, Lakatos' considerations regarding scientific research programmes, and Kuhn's constructivism and continuing up to recent approaches such as van Fraassen's constructive empiricism, or Boyd's naturalism, the debate has produced a large amount of quite fruitful results. During this development, new aspects of scientific research in general, as well as scientific theories in particular, have been envisaged and discussed continuously. As a result, we are endowed today with a richer and much more differentiated picture of science than ever before. In our view, the enduring vividness of the debate is not, as Rorty wants us to believe, due to its inability to solve problems and its overall fruitlessness. Rather, it shows its enormous practical significance and the permanent enrichment it gives to science by introducing new ideas of great interest for scientists which are worth discussing in the scientific communities. Particularly in the light of recent developments in the realism/antirealism debate, it seems plausible to adopt an optimistic stance towards the solution of at least some of the debate's most fundamental questions. Why should we wish to get rid of a theoretically fruitful and action-guiding tradition of philosophical problems?

More importantly, however, we do not regard it as the main task of philosophy to solve or dissolve problems, but, quite the opposite, to develop conceptual frameworks and theoretical problems that lead to further vivid and fruitful discussions. We think that the development of problems as such can be a very fruitful activity, as it opens new perspectives on a certain topic

10   Cf. ibid., p. 115 and PRM 45.

and thereby helps us to bring into view different aspects of it. Moreover, the establishment of new methods and approaches is very often due to the acceptance of a problematic setting. In sum, being occupied with complex philosophical problems rather increases than diminishes man's creativity.

As a consequence of this consideration, we do not understand Rorty in his desire to abandon the idea of truth as a goal for philosophy. The pursuit of truth seems to be an essential aspect of intellectual fantasy and creativity. A further consideration that can be put forth in favor of the relevance of the realism/antirealism debate is of pragmatic character. Obviously, many people feel a strong need for pursuing truth. Rorty's recommendation is to simply forget about such philosophical inclinations, as they are likely to lead to a dogmatic, anti-liberalist view. But can Rorty decide which needs are *good* and should therefore be satisfied, and which are the *bad* ones we should forget about?

Moreover, giving up absolute truth as a guiding idea seems to lead to relativism. Rorty himself does not want to be a relativist and tries to avoid it by invoking the idea of ethnocentrism. According to ethnocentrism we should try to find out what truth means for us, i. e., in the context of our culture or society, and not what it could mean universally. From an ethnocentrist point of view truth can only be construed as »acceptability to *us* at our best«. (PRM 52.) However, it seems to be unclear whether the ethnocentrist move can prevent Rorty from embracing relativism. To believe that truth can only be the truth of a particular community or culture simply amounts to cultural relativism. Accepting the values of one's culture and, at the same time, acknowledging that these values are dependent on contingent cultural developments obviously results in a cynical position in the uneasy neighborhood of relativism.[11]

---

11   Susan Haack made a somewhat similar point. She characterizes Rorty's position as cynical, »because if one really believed that criteria of justification are purely conventional, wholly without objective grounding, then, though one might conform to the justification practices of one's own epistemic community, one would be obliged to adopt an attitude of cynicism towards them, to think of justification always in covert square quotes. ... [O]ne cannot coherently engage fully – non-cynically – in a practice of justifying beliefs that one regards as wholly conventional. For to believe that p is to accept p as true.« (Haack 1993, p. 193-194.)

Contrary to Rorty's advice, philosophy should be considered as a special way of life that includes a passionate desire to solve philosophical problems rather than rejoicing in their total dissolution. Those taking part in philosophical debates are not bored by troublesome problems, but rather with the lacking of problems to be solved!

Let us formulate a final statement: We happily invite everyone to join the debate on realism and antirealism and beg philosophers not to be blinded by rash and seemingly viable dissolutions of hard problems. We hope that the promising project of philosophy that began millennia ago can be continued. Perhaps even Rorty's philosophy might help with this. We refuse however to abandon philosophical debates simply on the ground that old challenges like the quest for truth and realism have yet to be met.

References

Cherniak, Christopher 1981. »Minimal Rationality«, in: *Mind* 90, p. 161-183.

Davidson, Donald 1984a. »Truth and Meaning«, in: *Inquiries Into Truth and Interpretation*, Oxford: Clarendon Press, p. 17-36.

Davidson, Donald 1984b. »Radical Interpretation«, in: *Inquiries Into Truth and Interpretation*, Oxford: Clarendon Press, p. 125-139.

Davidson, Donald 1984c. »On the Very Idea of a Conceptual Scheme«, in: *Inquiries Into Truth and Interpretation*, Oxford: Clarendon Press, p. 183-198.

Devitt, Michael 1987. »Rorty's Mirrorless World«, in: *Midwest Studies in Philosophy* 12, p. 157-177.

Fine, Arthur 1986. »The Natural Ontological Attitude«, in: *The Shaky Game. Einstein, Realism, and Quantum Theory*, Chicago: Univ. of Chicago Press, p. 112-135.

Haack, Susan 1993. »Vulgar Pragmatism. An Unedifying Prospect«, in: *Evidence and Inquiry*, Oxford: Blackwell, p. 182-202.

Henderson, David K. 1987. »The Principle of Charity and the Problem of Irrationality (Translation and the Problem of Irrationality)«, in: *Synthese* 73, p. 225-252.

IS RORTY'S NON-REDUCTIVE NATURALISM REDUCTIVE?

Attila Karakuş and Andreas Vieth

ABSTRACT: Naturalism is an antidualist and antiessentialist philosophy. Richard Rorty describes himself as non-reductive naturalist by claiming that we should not abandon the language game of the mental. But he monopolizes the observer perspective while giving up the participant perspective. We define naturalism as a philosophical position founded on three egalitarian theses: (1) ontological monism, (2) methodological scientism and (3) epistemological secularism. While Rorty is consequently egalitarian with respect to ontology his behaviorism is antiegalitarian with respect to methodology. We distinguish between strong naturalism (only ontological egalitarianism) and weak naturalism (threefold egalitarianism). Only the last position is compatible with wholehearted pragmatism.

KEYWORDS: naturalism, reductionism, scientism, behaviorism, pragmatism, participant perspective, observer perspective

0 INTRODUCTION

In this paper we want to deal with Richard Rorty's notion of *naturalism*. Our aim is to point to some reductive consequences of his philosophy which may stand in contrast to his own explicit intentions. (1) We *first* give a brief overview of what we think are the core features of naturalism in his philosophy. We generally follow him in advocating both pragmatism and naturalism, however, we will suggest some conceptual clarifications. (2) We *secondly* scrutinize especially his advocacy of behaviorism as one central aspect of his naturalist conception of the mind. With respect to this we try to distinguish two kinds of philosophical naturalism. The first option is *strong naturalism* which is to be associated with behaviorism. We will argue that this version seems to be reductive insofar as it repudiates the participant perspective and the manifest image of the world.[1] Against this we propose a *weak* version of naturalism which is in our view a non-reductive position. In the following section we anticipate an argument Rorty might state. (3) Weak naturalism's willingness to accept the manifest image of the world – which is as intimate from a pragmatist perspective as the scientific image – might provoke the counter-attack that consciousness and other genuine mental phenomena and their conceptual counterparts in philosophy revive bad metaphysics. Certainly we cannot oppose this argument directly for we cannot develop a conception of the mental which corresponds to weak naturalism. We try to argue indirectly. We don't think that naturalism is incompatible with the idea of intrinsicality. There may be something like the contingent-constitutive or hypothetically necessary phenomena between the necessity and the eternal on the one hand and the contingent on the other. (4) Certainly we do not want to suggest anti-behaviorism as our proposal for the philosophy of mind. Our aim in this paper is narrower. In the concluding part we suggest that there are pragmatic reasons not to plead for behaviorism and therefore to avoid reductionism. Our suspicion is that either Rorty's conception of mind may be irreconcilable with his own pragmatic attitudes or we need some clarification why one should defend what we call *strong naturalism*.

1   RORTY'S NATURALISM: THE CORE FEATURES

In characterizing his conception of naturalism the first thing to take into account is that in the philosophical tradition the notion »naturalism« is often

---

1   The opposition of the manifest and the scientific image of the world is a topic discussed by Sellars (cf. 1963). Traditional philosophy is a refinement and endorsement of the manifest image of man-in-the-world (p. 8). The scientific image is both a methodological refinement of the manifest image and a rival (p. 20). The clash between both consists in the fact that same entities in the manifest image are not intersubjectively accessible (i. e. observable): »[E]ach scientific theory is ... a structure« which is built ... within the intersubjectively accessible world of perceptible things« (p. 20). Therefore scientific psychology has to proceed behavioristically (p. 22). Sellars solution of the clash of images is not to reconcile both, but to join the manifest to the scientific (ibid., p. 40). – In Sellars, therefore, there is a comparable tendency to reductivism as in Rorty. For another solution of the clash of both images cf. Quante 2000.

used interchangeably at least with »physicalism«, »materialism« or »ontological monism«. Therefore, we have to clarify in what sense Rorty can be reasonably called a naturalist. To begin with it is easier to characterize his position indirectly. He disassociates from what he calls *metaphysics*, something that according to him is to be identified with both *essentialism* and *dualism*. Conversely his naturalism stems from two strong philosophical motivations: *anti-essentialism* and *anti-dualism*.

With the denial of essentialism Rorty wants to abandon the traditional idea that there may be something or some qualities which are non-contingent. According to him, we should ultimately give up the idea that the things have a *nature* in the philosophical sense of *essence*. Neither the mental nor the physical do have essential or necessary traits. On the contrary, all things are contingent. Anti-essentialism therefore amounts to the thesis that the distinction between *accidence* and *substance* is nonsense. And with the denial of any sort of *substance-dualism* he associates the reconciliation of the mental and the material. So, in addition, naturalism implies an ontological thesis which he sets against inherited philosophical Platonism, Cartesianism and other positions which were of cultural dominance at least in the European history of ideas. – Both of these philosophical intuitions are to be found ubiquitously in his writings. To underline this we would like to cite only one passage:

> [Antidualist philosophers try to] shake of the influence of characteristic metaphysical dualisms, which the philosophical traditions of the occident inherited from the Greeks. Namely dualisms of accident, substance and property, appearance and reality. They endeavor to displace a world-view moulded out of these contrasting concepts by a vision of a flux of constantly changing relations which do not exist between solid relata but between relations.[2]

2   [Antidualistische Philosophen versuchen,] »den Einfluss der spezifisch metaphysischen Dualismen abzuschütteln [...], die die philosophische Tradition des Abendlands von den Griechen geerbt hat, also die Dualismen zwischen Wesen und Akzidenz, Substanz und Eigenschaft, Erscheinung und Wirklichkeit. Sie bemühen sich um die Verdrängung des mit Hilfe dieser Gegensatzpaare konstruierten Weltbildes durch ein Bild von einem Strom ständig wechselnder Beziehungen, und zwar Beziehungen, die nicht zwischen festen Relata bestehen, sondern zwischen Beziehungen« (WSW 37, own translation).

Richard Rorty is therefore a naturalist philosopher in so far as he tries to shake off the influence of the specific metaphysical dualisms within the philosophical tradition. While naturalism should not be identified with the natural sciences – such as physics or biology –, the paradigm of modern philosophical anti-essentialism and anti-dualism owes much to them in penetrating our culture. Particularly in the first part of his highly influential book *Philosophy and the Mirror of Nature* we find an attempt both to explain the »genealogy« of the dualistic and essentialist intuitions and to avoid them in modern philosophy. Now, we would like to point at a central methodological thesis. Again in *Philosophy and the Mirror of Nature* it is obvious that his naturalism is deeply connected with an admiration of science, especially the natural sciences: Bad metaphysics is »the attempt to give knowledge of what science cannot know« (PMN 384). It has to be extirpated. Good metaphysics[3] in contrast is based on three aspects of conceptual egalitarianism we find frequently in his philosophy:

(1)   The *ontological* egalitarianism (*substance monism*): There is no meaningful talk of a supernatural substance.[4] There is – in whatever sense – only one

3   As with terms like »naturalism«, »anti-naturalism«, »supra-naturalism« and so on we use the term »metaphysics« in a neutral, non-polemic sense. A position directed against (bad) metaphysics because of its dualism and essentialism is itself a (good) metaphysical position for which anti-dualism and anti-essentialism are constitutive conceptual features.

4   John Dewey distinguishes two versions of anti-naturalism of which supra-naturalism (the belief in a higher and/or divine realm of being) is only one. The other is directed against science in general: »Democracy cannot obtain adequate recognition of its own meaning or coherent practical realization as long as antinaturalism operates to delay and frustrate the use of the methods by which alone understanding and consequent ability to guide social relationships are attained« (cf. Dewey 1944, p. 3). These so-called extranaturalists are »rationalist« philosophers (or religious thinkers like creationists etc.) who reject democratic progress which is enlightened from science: »Students of this subject (i. e. philosophy of language), who regard themselves as antimetaphysical scientific positivists, nevertheless write as if words consisted of an ›inner‹ private, mentalistic core or substance and an ›outer‹ physical shell by means of which a ›subjective‹ intrinsically incommunicable somehow gets conveyed ›trans-subjectively‹« (ibid., p. 4). Certainly there are rational-foundationalist thinkers which are in questions of moral or ethical justification orientated towards universal norms etc. Our suspicion is that Dewey confuses their advocacy of a particular set

reality.

(2) The *methodological* egalitarianism: Only science reveals knowledge of this reality. Concerning this reality there is no »higher« way or procedure to knowledge.

(3) The *epistemological* egalitarianism: Knowledge should be built on empirical experience of this reality and not with reference to supernatural paths of cognition.

We think that his position takes the shape of an endeavor of demarcating philosophy from bad metaphysics. (Cf. Dennes 1944, esp. p. 293.) Good metaphysics may be labeled as deeply egalitarian: Whatever exists or may be called real in whatever sense, it exists in the same sense and is equally real as everything else. There is one reality: In its totality this reality is constituted pragmatically. *Pragmatic Realism* is not the position that there is an independent reality, but that acting persons have the feeling that there *are* differences in their practice. These differences constitute the realm of being. Ontological egalitarianism is not committed to the idea of a reality independent of human practice. The dominant feature of this one reality is that everything is equally good or bad and that there is no higher department in this reality. From his pragmatic viewpoint everything may be called real and therefore be part of our world which is constituted by practical differences or insofar as it is of practical relevance. (Cf. IR, NRP, PRM.) But the approach of good metaphysics sketched so far is vague and has to be refined. In what follows, we argue that Rorty seems to go too far in his naturalist efforts to make more explicit what good metaphysics is.

of material values and their positions concerning ethical justification with the question of naturalism and theory of science. If this is right such terms as »naturalist«, »supra-naturalist« and »extra-naturalist« are used in Dewey 1944 in a polemic way. In what follows we argue mainly on the basis of Dewey 1927 and therefore use these terms without moralistic connotations.

2   RORTY'S NON-REDUCTIVE NATURALISM

In his essay *Non-Reductive Physicalism* Rorty intends to elaborate – with the help
of Donald Davidson's philosophy – a »picture of the relations between the
human self and the world which, though ›naturalized‹ through and through,
excludes nothing« (113). Rorty wants to be a naturalist in another, a non-reductive sense: In other words, the natural sciences do not provide us a privileged access to the world. That is the reason why we called good metaphysics
naturalism and not *physicalism*. The core feature of reductive versions of naturalism is to deny that the realm of mental or cultural phenomena may be en-
closed in our concept of reality. The reductive concept of reality restricts entities which are allowed to be real to the ontological inventory of e. g. physics.
One argument against such reductive positions is that we as pragmatists have
the intuition that e. g. culture or the mental are real just because in our practice we make differences.[5] Reductionism (or scientism) threatens egalitarian
aspects of naturalism mainly by restricting the pragmatic broader concept of
reality.

Language games of the cultural sphere – for which Rorty argues –
should enjoy the same rights as physical or biological talk. Our mentalist talk
should be equally legitimate as our talk of atoms in the void. We should therefore plead for a plurality of egalitarian language games. Only pragmatic reasons that are in the same way relative to language let us prefer the one language game to another. In our biography we have accepted culturally and historically contingent norms of conditions for the application of different
language games. Pragmatic reasons for distinction and justified application of
a specific talk are in particular appropriateness, success, and efficiency, but
also upbringing, social and historical influences. As we agree with Rorty that
good metaphysics should be ontologically, methodologically and epistemolo-

5   We do not agree with Rorty that Davidson's central thesis of non-reductive physical-
    ism is right: »that a given event can be described equally well in physiological and
    psychological, nonintentional and intentional, terms« (NRP 114). From a pragmatic
    point of view we have reasons to choose one or the other description. And these
    reasons are not arbitrary. In the sense that one description is apt *hic et nunc* and the
    other is unsuitable. To say that they are »equally well« can be regarded as true only if
    one looses contact to practice.

gically *egalitarian* we also approve of his insistence that naturalism should be non-reductive. We interpret this argument as directed towards a consequent adherence to ontological egalitarianism.[6]

Naturalism as a threefold egalitarian conception is the position that our conception of reality should be scientific as opposed to supernaturalism. But now we get into difficulties and perhaps we do not further agree with Rorty. As a result of the non-reductiveness of his naturalism we are justified to use mental predicates in vernacular talk about intentions, emotions, beliefs, reasons, qualia, first-person-perspective and so on. But we have to do this in a scientific manner. Now we have to face a crucial decision if we want to explicate our scientific conception of mental phenomena or predicates. Rorty demands that our scientific talk of mental phenomena and accordingly mental predicates pursue *behaviorist* methods.[7] The core of behaviorism is to deny that there is a special aspect of what we usually call the mental which is usually called participant perspective. Correspondingly his behaviorist move is due to a sincere *observer perspective*. Therefore, we now suggest to distinguish *strong* and *weak naturalism*.[8]

6   Rorty argues against the reductionist version of naturalism. Such a position adds to the thesis that there are two or more language games the further thesis that one of these languages is nothing more than the other. The reductionist conclusion is: therefore we do not really need one of these language games. Rorty refuses it. (Cf. e. g. NRP 115, 121.) One can therefore conclude from a pragmatist viewpoint: Reductionism is false because we need both language games (each and them both in contrast with each other). They are useful to us even they are learned and culturally contingent. Antireductionism is therefore an ontological thesis in the pragmatist sense that there *really* are practical differences which are constituted by us using the language games following rules.

7   Cf. e. g. NRP (esp. 121, 123), IR 109 f., and PMN, chap. 1, 2.4, 2.6.

8   The distinction follows loosely Dewey's distinction of half- and wholehearted naturalism in a discussion with Santayana (cf. Dewey 1927, Santayana 1925 and DM). Dewey argues for a plurality of »perspectives« which do not stamp their own inner laws on one another and therefore are *equal* legitimate. Rorty does not accept e. g. consciousness or first-person-perspective (NRP 123, DDI 99 f.) for reasons we would arrange as follows: Mental perspective implies fore- and background or an »inner eye« seeing and in seeing constituting what Santayana calls »the dominance of the foreground« (Santayana 1925, p. 251). Santayana replies: »In nature there is no foreground or background, no here, no now, no moral cathedra, no centre so really central as to reduce all other things to mere margins and mere perspectives.« And Naturalism is abandoned respectively bad metaphysics accepted if philosophy gets to

(A) *Strong naturalism* is the thesis that good metaphysics is not compatible
with the philosophical acceptance of a participant perspective. The conception of scientific knowledge should include only such entities which
are observable in the sense that they are accessible to everyone directly
and in the same way.

(B) *Weak naturalism* is the thesis that good metaphysics is compatible with
philosophical acceptance of a participant perspective. It accuses strong
naturalism as reductive, because it is not compatible with our ordinary
live experience.

We said that Rorty – due to his pragmatism – wants us to accept that all the
different language games are equally justified (recognized). None of them is
superior to another one. Now he holds on to the mental insofar as he recog-
nizes that there is something we call »mental«. As we said above, we follow
him in his denial of bad metaphysics which postulates a mental substance.
The main reason for this is that according to substance-dualism of Cartesian
provenance we do not have empirical knowledge of the mental substance.
From a Platonic viewpoint the supernatural realm of the mental is higher and
morally better than the rest of the universe. This, too, is incompatible with a
naturalistic conception of science.

In his behaviorist turn Rorty challenges our ordinary life experience.[9] We
assume to have knowledge of our reasons for actions, of pain, and of intentions of which we sometimes say that they are reasons for actions. And we
think that we at least sometimes have better access to some explanatory
factors of our behavior and other aspects of our mental life because we participate in it. The »we« includes not only philosophers but also persons who

like the foreground (ibid. 251 f.). Perhaps a philosophy like Cartesianism likes the
foreground too much but this is no argument to totally abandon it. Maybe Rorty argues in the direction of Santayana in NRP and DDI (and elsewhere). But we would
regard this as erroneous because the argument rests on the assumption that what is
an entity in one perspective (language game) has at least possibly to be fully reconstructed in another perspective (language game). But Santayana is right: in the nature
of some natural sciences (physics, chemistry) there is nothing comparable to »foreground«. We hold the premise false for it deprives both perspectives of *equal* entitle-
ment in favor of the perspective of physics and chemistry (as much as bad metaphysics does in favor of the mental).

9   That he is conscious of this difficulty one can find e. g. in NRP 123.

have never come across good or bad metaphysics. Why should pragmatic versions of (the concept of) scientific knowledge not accept genuine talk of mental entities? What is Rorty's argument for this behaviorist turn against the participant perspective in his concept of scientific knowledge?

First of all his behaviorism concerning the conceptualization of the mental is a result of his anti-dualist and anti-essentialist attitude. In his view, any »realistic« interpretation leads to ontological dualism. Those who use concepts like »reason«, »consciousness« or »qualia« and the first-person-perspective in order to examine the nature of the properties of mind are suspected of employing ontologically bad metaphysical commitments. Behaviorism provides seemingly a solution: We can offer conceptions of mental phenomena in addition to non-mental phenomena and therefore in Rorty's eyes save our ordinary mentalistic talk *even if* we abandon the participant perspective.

Now, in our view, this contradicts the epistemological thesis of good naturalism. The reason for this is that the participant perspective is a genuine kind of empirical experience – at least if we observe our own evidence of our own inner life.[10] (We certainly cannot offer here a theory of the mental. But that is not necessary for our argument.) Every person thinks to have empirical evidence of his or her so-called *inner life* even if this is in part accessible only from a participant perspective. Are there reasons for discrediting this empirical experience in the context of naturalistic theory and good metaphysics? We think that Rorty's philosophy provides us with two lines of argument:

(1) First, the argument that he supplies us is a *slippery-slope-argument*.[11] It means briefly that if a presupposition (necessarily) leads to something

10   Krikorian 1944 indicates that entities which presuppose participant perspective often also have another side, which is observable. We do not have direct consciousness of the desires of other selves but we have behavioral indicators which signal us some aspects which would convince us when another person says that she has a desire to do or get something. Psychology likewise has objective criteria for convincing reports of inner states which persons reveal. But these criteria presuppose command of the participant perspective on the side of the observing scientist. Science then is in some continuity with our everyday pragmatic access to mental states of others. As Krikorian writes: »In maintaining that mind as conation is anticipatory there is no intention of introducing a break into the continuity of nature« (ibid.). Cf. Dewey 1927, p. 76: »Experience ... constitutes ... a foreground. But it is a foreground *of* nature. ... the foreground is itself a portion of nature, an integral portion ...«.

unacceptable, then it is to be dismissed. And Rorty seems to think that if philosophers deny that mentalistic talk is only a *façon de parler* and therefore offer *genuine* concepts for mental phenomena and entities, then we cannot avoid slipping into bad metaphysics. In our view, this is at least not a strong argument. One can doubt if it is an argument at all, for the ordinary-life-experience is not slipping automatically into bad metaphysics – at least not without helping philosophers. (We will come back to this line of argument in the next section.)

(2) Second, and more interestingly, in the conceptual framework of naturalism we can find argumentative resources: namely, the methodological thesis mentioned above. If we say that knowledge should be founded in scientific method then his rejection of the participant perspective may use the following argument: Empirical experience as the basis of scientific knowledge is gained only through something like *scientific experiments* which take place under explicit control of circumstances in which they are reproducible anywhere, at any time and by any person. If we limit the concept of *naturalistic experience* to experiments in natural sciences then certainly a non-behaviorist conception of the mental is bad metaphysics. But why should we?

Perhaps there is a convincing answer to this question. Nevertheless, we would say that we should characterize Rorty's naturalism as *strong* then, considering that his conception of naturalism is close to the concept of nature which is mainly characteristic for the natural sciences. If Rorty advocates strong naturalism instead of weak naturalism he – in our opinion – leaves the ground of the pragmatic conception of experience.[12] In this respect we take his non-reductive naturalism to be reductive. Against this position we will offer a little example of a pragmatic argument for weak naturalism in the last section. In the following section we want to scrutinize the »slippery slope« into bad metaphysics.

11   WSW 62 (advantage of anti-essentialism is that – if accepted – many philosophical problems vanish because they cannot formulated anymore), and with respect to philosophy of mind PMN, cp. 1.6, and p. 126.
12   This seems to be the Dewey's aim when he argues for »half-hearted naturalism« (cf. 1927). »Whole-hearted naturalism« is not »consequently pursued naturalism« but »reductionism« or »scientism«.

3   Slippery Slope: The Supposed
Necessity of Bad Metaphysics

At this point we have to anticipate a possible objection. Perhaps, Rorty's advocacy of behaviorism is only meant to provoke philosophers to think about the antinaturalist consequences of their mentalist talk.[13] And maybe most philosophers really cannot control themselves in falling back into antinaturalist philosophy when conceptually accepting »the mental« as opposed to »the physical«. But this kind of slippery slope should not be taken serious. Nevertheless in our context there is another version of this kind of argument. The manner of *speaking* of a »first-person-perspective«, in Rortys eyes, necessarily leads to the conceptual commitment that there are intrinsic features. And in his article *Daniel Dennett on Intrinsicality* Rorty argues that this is to abandon naturalism, because intrinsicality is nothing but a last refuge of dualism (DDI 110).

> The cash value of the term ›first-person point of view‹, as it is used by Nagel, Searle, and others, is: a point of view that produces knowledge of *intrinsic*, nonrelational properties of mental events (DDI 99).

Consciousness, first-person-perspective and other concepts of the philosophy of *the* mental are accused to imply philosophical positions which offend against the antiessentialist and antimetaphysicalist motivations of Rorty's philosophy.

> But once we drop the notion of ›consciousness‹ there is no harm in continuing to speak of a distinct entity called ›the self‹ which consists of the

---

13   For a good characterization of behaviorism in this *philosophical* context cf. Sellars 1963, p. 22 f. We think that this is the way »behaviorism« as a concept is used in Santayana 1925, p. 257, and Dewey 1927, p. 79, and in NRP. The core of philosophical behaviorism is not to deny the existence or reality of mind and the usefulness of mentalistic concepts referring to it, but restrict existence and usefulness »scientifically« (cf. footnote 1).

mental states of the human being: her beliefs, desires, moods, etc. The important thing is to think of the collection of those things as *being* the self rather than as something which the self *has*. The latter notion is a leftover of the traditional Western temptation to model thinking on vision, and to postulate an ›inner eye‹ which inspects inner states (NRP 123).

It is nearly the same point for which Santayana criticizes Dewey's »Half-Hearted Naturalism« (Santayana 1925, p. 251, 255 f.). The point here seems to be that conceptually accepting the »privacy of the foreground« necessarily leads to dualism and essentialism. To speak of a foreground seems to recognize the inner eye of the Cartesian theatre as the self which (a) has knowledge of itself and (b) has to be distinguished form beliefs, emotions and so on. The self is not to be identified with its changing contents and independent of these contents the self has immediate knowledge of itself which is not acquired through biographical experience and contact with the outer world. Therefore there is a version of a slippery slope which should be taken serious because it claims conceptual necessity. Against this Dewey points out that one must consider a difference:

> I repeat, then, that I hold that everything which is experienced *has* immediacy, and that I also hold that every natural existence, in its own unique and brutal particularity of existence, also *has* immediacy, so that the immediacy which characterizes things experienced is not specious, being neither an unnatural irruption nor a supernatural imposition. To *have* traits, however, is not to *be* them, certainly not in any exclusive sense (Dewey 1927, p. 77).

Dewey's argument seems to be the following: Experience constitutes a foreground but as a foreground of nature (Dewey 1927, p. 76). His view is that this does not lead – at least not with conceptual necessity – to antinaturalist tendencies in philosophy. Therefore the »I« who *has* immediate features in experience (e. g. pain) is real but it is not »a center of gravity« as conceived of it in the Cartesian theatre version of consciousness. (Dewey 1927, p. 78.) For the Cartesian self it is not central to *have* immediacy but to *be* immediate. In Cartesian mentalist talk we say »I have pain«. But this may not be interpreted as: »There are two things – the ›I‹ and ›pain‹ – and the one has the other«. While having pain is »nexonial« (the self gets into contact with the corporeal and empirically perceived world and with itself in former conditions) the self is immediate. Therefore, there are two kinds of immediacies: the bodily or corporeal of entities described by natural sciences and the mental of consciousness or the foreground. And to accept both means to demand that it is impossible to convert them mutually without any loss: The manifest and the scientific image are equally basic and irreducible. To accept mentalist and naturalist/physicalist talk should imply to accept two kinds of immediacies just as it should imply acceptance of one realm of being (without something being immediate) but two kinds of epistemic access (participant and observer perspective). This halfhearted naturalism is not a fallback into dualism. (At least, not with conceptual necessity.) We interpret Dewey's position in this way:

(1) Santayana restricts the notion of reality to those entities which are accessible from the observer perspective. His notion of reality is moulded out of methodological constraints of natural sciences. What is real is accessible from the viewpoint of natural sciences. And: These entities *are* reality. But exclusiveness is no longer only methodologically but also ontologically. And therefore strong naturalism is (as is dualism) a wrong (or at least not a philosophically necessary) ontological thesis.[14]

(2) Dewey is naturalist in that he ontologically accepts only one realm of reality. But this realm is accessible from two mutually exclusive methodologies (i. e. two perspectives). Therefore there are two realities with respect to methodology but only one with regard to ontology. Weak natur-

14   The objects of exclusiveness and dominance at this point of argument are important: »... how comes it that Dewey has a metaphysics of his own ...? This question ... may be answered ... in a single phrase: *The dominance of the foreground.* In nature there is no foreground or background ...« (Santayana 1925, p. 251). The term »nature« in this quotation is the object of natural sciences. It is not the object of the pragmatist version of nature: »Naturalism is a primary system, or rather it is not a special system at all, but the spontaneous and inevitable body of beliefs involved in animal life« (Santayana 1925, p. 245). The concept of nature in this »primary« (i. e. prephilosophically) sense is moulded out of two perspectives without any *non-contingent* dominance. To accept foreground is not necessary to accept its dominance.

alism is ontological monism with a double *face*.

One has to decide whether one would like to be a wholehearted pragmatist (weak naturalism) or a wholehearted naturalist (strong naturalism). The double face of weak naturalism indeed implies intrinsicality in the sense of intrinsic inwardness and non-contingence. As we said above we cannot explicate in more detail the concept of experience, the self, and of *the* mental suitable to weak naturalism. Nevertheless we would like to roughly touch on two central features to clear weak naturalism of antinaturalist suspicions.

(1) *Intrinsic inwardness*: The conscious self as an inner nucleus which has ineffable knowledge of itself and is foundation of all effable knowledge (DDI 101). The concept of the intrinsic self – which Rorty attributes to Nagel and Searle – is in its core non-relational and independent of biographical experience and development. Compensating the lack of theoretical concepts we would like to argue with examples: Our reports of pain-states are learned. Perhaps as young children we sometime said that we have a stomach-ache. Then the situation may be vague. On the one hand there is an inner certainty to the child of feeling unwell (we provide that young children's reports are sincere). But parents know that the report is sometimes highly dubious because children have to learn: Maybe the child has a headache, is hungry or anxious etc. Biographically it has to learn to give correct reports of inner states. Consciousness of these inner states develops depending on this process. Later in life we comment our actions by telling stories about our motives. Sometimes other persons accept our reports because of their evidence of our behavior. Sometimes they correct our reports by rightly informing us what our real motives are and we learn from them. – None of both perspectives may be isolated from the other conceptually (neither is the conscious self a spontaneous source of infallible and ineffable knowledge ...), and dominance of one is only passing and due to contingent conditions (... nor is one side the foundation of the other).

(2) *Non-Contingence*: Contingence is one of the deepest and central experiences of modern times. It is one task of natural sciences to show in what ways everything is contingent. Personal ways of life and social institu-

tions are culturally and historically contingent too. One can agree with this diagnosis, but deny that everything is contingent every time and everywhere in every sense. Human beings as animals are evolutionarily contingent. There were and perhaps will be times without humans. But if there are humans then some features in the world are necessary: e. g. that there are animals which are in need of an especially human mixture of nutritional substances. And if there are humans there is love, hate, economy, cultural activity etc. Therefore there is something intermediate between universal necessity and non-contingence that we may call the *contingent-constitutive* or *hypothetical-necessity*.

All in all our arguments are weak because they are mainly negative and sketchy. They do not provide a conceptually clear position. We think that Richard Rorty is right in his advocacy for naturalism and in his antidualist and antiessentialist intuitions. The last implies a sound philosophical caution concerning traditional concepts of »intrinsicality« and »non-contingence« which he expresses in »Daniel Dennett on Intrinsicality« and elsewhere. But we are hesitant to accept that this caution requires philosophers to advocate for (what we call) strong naturalism. We hold that there is no conceptual necessity that is responsible for (what we call) weak naturalism slipping into bad metaphysics.

4 ADVOCATING WEAK NATURALISM

Rorty assigns himself to pragmatism. From a pragmatic point of view everything may be called real which makes a practical difference. Reality in this sense is not independent from practice, but it is an aspect of the experience of acting persons. We therefore may be entitled to argue for a plurality of departments of reality and corresponding sections of genuine knowledge. This assumption is valid even if we have to acknowledge that the plurality of language games and the sections of knowledge next to one another involve severe contradictions in our self-image. Even a duality of language games and sections of knowledge may be contradictory: As persons we are physical-mental-entities. Some aspects of us are accessible directly via introspection and others are not. As persons we know that we must change our point of view from participating to observing, depending on the contingent requests of challenging situations. From a pragmatic point of view this is our human condition. Sometimes both aspects get in severe practical dilemmas which we have to cope with.

Both perspectives – the third- and the first-person-perspective – have practical consequences for our understanding of ourselves and the world. Hence there should be no problem for pragmatists to take the intentional vocabulary and the corresponding phenomena as much as »real« as the non-intentional. The concept of *health* for example is split into two aspects: Sometimes we are ill or healthy viewed from an observer perspective, but ill from our participating viewpoint. Sometimes it is vice versa. Sometimes our blood count is very bad. Then we are objectively ill. Assuming that our physician and the laboratory have done their job well we are ill. This is valid even if we feel well and live a hundred years with this blood count. Sometimes our blood count is very good. Then we are objectively healthy but we may nonetheless feel very bad. Perhaps we die soon as objectively healthy persons. To put it short health is a psychosomatic concept which has a duality of aspects some of which are accessible directly via introspection and consciousness, others via observation and experiment. It is crucial to the concept of health that we need both perspectives. Taking one or the other perspective makes a pragmatic difference in medicine. And it is important that a pragmatic concept of experience offers countless phenomena and concepts which reveal this practically constructive duality. In everyday life this antagonistic nature of concepts is as useful as it is inevitable. Especially *persons* regard themselves in this antagonistic way as mental and physical entities without any »natural« tendency to conceive of this dichotomy in terms of ›philosophical systems inherited from the Greeks‹. A whole-hearted pragmatism therefore has to accept half-hearted naturalism.

We argue that Rorty's naturalism is reductive because he extends the methodological rules of the natural sciences to our *manifest image of the world* as such (strong naturalism). His own anti-reductionism only compensates the ontological anti-egalitarianism of naturalistic scientism. The result is a purely scientific image of the world. Concerning methodological and epistemological aspects of naturalism Rorty seems to recall traditional anti-egalitarian intuitions of »whole-hearted« naturalism. We use his advocacy of epistemological behaviorism as evidence for this diagnosis. But this seems to be bad metaphysics of the new naturalistic philosophy. Since, at least for a pragmatic philosophical account it does make a difference whether phenomena are knowable from observation or from a participating conscious sight. (This metaphysics is bad because methodological principles determine what is ontologically allowed to be called »real«.)

And we often need two (or perhaps more) perspectives supplementing each other constructively and antagonistically in our manifest image of the world. To restrict the conception of knowledge to our *scientific image of the world* is a reductivist position. Rorty provides a philosophical reconstruction of the natural sciences' freeing themselves from metaphysical conclusions. He extends this position even against traditional bad metaphysics. The result is a kind of naturalism based mainly on egalitarian motives in ontological respects. We follow him on this, but our advocacy of weak naturalism is directed against his supposed methodological and epistemological anti-egalitarianism which restricts our concept of experience in a non-pragmatic manner.[15] Wholehearted good metaphysics is naturalist in a weak sense. Therefore we conclude that in naturalism one should accept a plurality of methodological approaches on which knowledge is based. This is due to the fact that the experience of acting persons has several departments which are based on differing methods of cognition. Against this background, epistemological behaviorism leads to a philosophically motivated impoverishment of human experience. And against this we advocate a wholehearted version of pragmatism.

15　In the preceding discussion we neglected epistemological egalitarianism because reductive naturalisms most important motive is preference for natural science as a methodology. Epistemological egalitarianism is only the theses, that we do not have a »special« sense (e. g. transcendental reason) which brings us into contact with a non-contingent »reality«. It is compatible with epistemological »aspect-dualism«. It is compatible with naturalism to postulate two senses or sensibilities in the way of admitting two images (manifest/scientific) or perspectives (participant/observer). This is not a violation of naturalist egalitarianism if one avoids badly ontologizing corresponding faculties. This is conceptually guaranteed if both views or perspectives are integrated into, correlated in or back traced to one »original view« (cf. Sellars 1963).

REFERENCES

Dennes, William R. 1944. »The Categories of Naturalism«, in: *Naturalism and the Human Spirit*, ed. by Yervant Houannes Krikorian, New York: Columbia Univ. Pr., S. 270-294.

Dewey, John 1927. »Half-Hearted Naturalism«, in: *Journal of Philosophy* 24, p. 57-64, reprinted in: *John Dewey, The Later Works, 1925-1953*, vol. 3, ed. by Ann Boydston, Carbondale, Edwardsville: Southern Illinois Univ. Pr., 1984, p. 73-81.

Dewey, John 1944. »Antinaturalism in Extremis«, in: *Naturalism and the Human Spirit*, ed. by Yervant Houannes Krikorian, New York: Columbia Univ. Pr., S. 1-16.

Krikorian, Yervant Houannes 1944. »A Naturalistic View of Mind«, in: *Naturalism and the Human Spirit*, ed. by Yervant Houannes Krikorian, New York: Columbia Univ. Pr., S. 242-269.

Quante, Michael 2000. »Manifest Versus Scientific Worldview. Uniting the Perspectives«, in: *Epistemologia* 23, p. 211-242.

Santayana, George 1925. »Dewey's Naturalistic Metaphysics«, in: Journal of Philosophy 22, p. 673-688, reprinted in: *The Philosophy of John Dewey*, ed. by Paul Arthur Schilpp, New York: Tudor Publ. Comp., 1939, p. 245-261.

Sellars, Wilfrid 1963. »Philosophy and the Scientific Image of Man«, in: *Science, Perception, and Reality*, London: Routledge and Kegan Paul, p. 1-40.

SKEPTICISM, CORRESPONDENCE, AND TRUTH

Nikola Kompa, Sebastian Muders,
Sebastian Schmoranzer, and Christian Weidemann

ABSTRACT: Rorty claims that it is an impossible task to answer the skeptic directly by first granting his premises and then arguing against his position. Instead of this, he tries to reject him indirectly, by doubting his premises and demonstrating (a) that the skeptic needs a correspondence theory of truth and (b), that such a theory is implausible. We grant that the skeptic at least needs a substantial notion of correspondence to make her point, but argue (i) that this notion is unproblematic given her needs and that (ii) Rorty's pragmatist reservations concerning this notion are unfounded.

KEYWORDS: Cartesian skepticism, truth, correspondence, tertia, facts, pragmatism

In his article »Antiskeptical Weapons: Michael Williams versus Donald Davidson« Richard Rorty agrees with Michael Williams that you cannot prove skeptical arguments wrong, incoherent or unintelligible. (AW 154 f.) Nonetheless it is still possible to repudiate the arguments as depending on highly theoretical and unnatural presuppositions one is not bound to accept.

Accordingly, Rorty does not claim that epistemological skepticism is wrong but rather that it is pointless. (AW 163, PDT 129, 134 f., 138.) Rorty adduces something like the following considerations for his claim:

P1: Skepticism is interesting only if you accept a correspondence theory of truth.

P2: One should not accept a correspondence theory of truth.

C: Therefore, skepticism is not interesting.[1]

---

1   PDT 129, 132-139, AW 163.

He offers no justification for the first premise. And his critique on substantial correspondence theories of truth is manifold. On the one hand it includes theoretical doubts concerning correspondence theories. On the other it comprises a pragmatist reservation concerning the usefulness of the notion of correspondence.

Before we scrutinize those arguments we would like to examine whether skepticism relies on a notion of truth as correspondence. In view of the large variety of skeptical positions we will confine ourselves to one form of skepticism, namely Cartesian skepticism.

1

The central feature of Cartesian skepticism lies in the so called skeptical hypotheses such as the dreaming hypothesis. The skeptic claims that we have knowledge about the external world only if we are able to exclude the dreaming hypothesis. But since our experience might be the same if we were dreaming as it is now, we cannot exclude the skeptical alternative. Therefore, we have no knowledge about the external world.

This line of reasoning presupposes that we would have no knowledge were the skeptical scenario true. But why is it, that I do not know that I have a hand if I only dream to have one? The point is that my access to the external world is blocked. My experience is thereby turned into an unreliable belief forming process since it is mere coincidence that my belief is true. Thus I am not justified in holding it.

Now, where does a substantial notion of truth enter the story? Could the skeptic not content himself, say, with a deflationist conception of truth? The vast majority of deflationist theories share the view that a sentence like »It is true that snow is white« could without harm be replaced by the sentence »Snow is white«. To attribute truth to a sentence is not to give any further information over and above what is already conveyed by the sentence itself.[2]

2   Deflationist theories might still diverge on whether we need the truth predicate at all. Redundancy theories à la Ramsey want to get rid of it whereas minimalist theories à la Horwich say that the predicate is still necessary for blind truth ascriptions such as »What Peter says is true« (Kirkham 1992, pp. 307-350).

Suppose the skeptic says: »We are not justified in believing it to be true that we have hands«. According to a deflationist theory, this amounts to nothing more than the phrase »We are not justified in believing that we have hands«. So what? The skeptic is fine with that. What interests the skeptic is not whether our belief has a property called »truth« but just whether we are justified in our opinion about the world. Briefly put: The skeptical argument is compatible with a deflationist theory of truth. Consequently the skeptic is not committed to any substantial notion of truth as correspondence.

But even so, a substantial notion of correspondence enters the skeptical argument all the same. In what sense are we not justified in believing that we have hands if we are only dreaming? Since in such a case our belief forming process about the external world is unreliable we are not justified in believing that our belief *corresponds* to the world. So, only if you care about whether our beliefs correspond to the world – and not for example whether they cohere with other beliefs – does Cartesian skepticism pose a threat. It is in this sense that Cartesian skepticism presupposes the notion of correspondence. Consequently Rorty's argument could be reformulated as follows:

P1: Cartesian skepticism is interesting only if you accept a substantial notion of correspondence between beliefs and the world.

P2: One should not accept such a notion.

C: Therefore, skepticism is not interesting.

But why should we not accept a notion of correspondence? This brings us back to Rorty's criticism of correspondence theories we want to scrutinize in the remaining part of the paper. First, we will concentrate on his theoretical critique of the notion of correspondence before, in a second step, we turn to his pragmatist reservations.

2

The notion of correspondence between beliefs and the world may seem suspicious for three reasons. First, one could doubt that there is any plausible item to be inserted on the belief-side of the correspondence relation. Secondly, one could find the relation itself unclear or dubious. And finally, one may have reservations concerning what it is that stands on the world-side of the correspondence relation. Rorty's criticism concerns each of these points.

In Rorty's eyes the skeptical argument rests on a notion of correspondence where the items on the belief-side of the relation imply the existence of so called tertia. Unfortunately, Rorty's use of the term »tertia« is far from clear since he subsumes a variety of different things under it, namely: intentional states, inner representations, a conceptual scheme, determinate meanings, what is before the speakers mind, a cultural tradition, a language and so on and so forth.[3] Now, what Rorty takes to be the essential characteristics of tertia seems to be the following: (A) tertia are something that can remain unchanged although the world changes dramatically. (B) they are something whose content we can know although we ignore its causes. (C) they are something standing between us and the world – whatever that means. (PDT 134, 138, 139, AW 160.)

Rorty's reasons why we should be suspicious of tertia are the following: First, the field linguist does not need them. So there is no reason to assume their existence. (PDT 138.) Secondly, tertia do not square well with an evolutionary theory of human nature. (ITGI 20.) Thirdly, getting rid of tertia helps us, among other things, to come to terms with the annoying problems of skepticism.[4] Fourthly, tertia are dubious entities.[5]

The argument against skepticism can then be stated thus: Cartesian skepticism implies the existence of tertia. Since there is no good reason to believe in their existence, there is no longer any reason to worry about the skeptical challenge. (PDT 139.)

Now, to what extent does the skeptical argument presume the existence of tertia? The story about the skeptical scenarios could be told as follows: Our beliefs are essentially determined by the neurological states of our brain and our language usage. Our beliefs could remain unchanged although the world changes radically because our neurological brain-states and our language usage can remain the same. Therefore it is always possible that our be-

---

3   PDT 132, 134, 136, 138, 139, 143, 147, ITGI 20, AW 160.
4   PDT 139. Rorty does not explicitly argue this way. But his remarks allow to interpret him like this.
5   This critique is only implicit in Rorty's writings.

liefs do not correspond to the world or that they correspond by mere coincidence. In a way, neurological states, linguistic usage and beliefs are tertia in Rorty's sense. They can remain unchanged although the world changes dramatically. Furthermore the skeptic assumes that we can have knowledge about our beliefs without knowing anything about their causes.

But how convincing are Rorty's arguments against tertia in this context? First, the only notion in the skeptical story the field linguist does not need is that of neurological brain-states. But that is no reason to doubt their existence. Science gives us good reasons not to. Secondly, an evolutionary theory of human nature has to explain our linguistic usage and the existence of brain-states and beliefs. If it failed to do so, this would be a reason against Darwinism and not against skepticism. Thirdly, skepticism will not be a problem if you do not accept the kind of tertia we are talking about. But now Rorty's argument against skepticism becomes circular in the following way: Skepticism can be repudiated because one should not accept the notion of tertia. And we should not accept this notion since thereby we can get rid of skepticism. Fourthly, what is so dubious about the notions of linguistic usage, brain-states and beliefs? Admittedly, the notion of belief stands in need of further clarification. But all the skeptic needs is this: (A) There is a notion of belief according to which our beliefs can remain unchanged although the world changes dramatically. (B) We can have knowledge about our beliefs although we are ignorant of their causes. A huge variety of theories of belief from identity theories to Cartesian theories can be conceived of in this way.

The only theory that does not comply with these requirements is an externalism about mental content – the view that beliefs and all other intentional mental states are to be individuated externally and thereby construed as having wide content.

According to externalism, you and your psychophysical twin on twin earth who has fallen victim to one of those skeptical scenarios do not share any beliefs about an external world at all. You and your twin share only those beliefs that are not susceptible to twin-earth-examples – if there are any.

But there may be good reasons not to subscribe to an externalism about mental content. For it seems to give way to a new form of skepticism – and not only skepticism about mental content, but also, and more importantly, to skepticism about our epistemic practice as such. If my beliefs have wide content, then their content is not necessarily accessible to me. But the content of my beliefs has to be accessible to me if my beliefs are to serve as reasons – reasons I can adduce in order to epistemically justify other beliefs and actions of mine. Our whole epistemic enterprise, the game of giving and asking for reasons, our demand for epistemic responsibility and so on, is based on the idea that the content of our beliefs is at least fairly accessible to us. So it seems that, at least for our epistemic purposes, our beliefs have to be individuated internally.[6] Let us sum up. The above discussion of Rorty's arguments against tertia shows that the arguments are not convincing. In a nutshell, the point is this: If the skeptical argument presupposes the existence of tertia then that kind of tertia is unproblematic.

3

So much for Rorty's attack against tertia. Let us now turn to his critique of the correspondence relation itself. His criticism concerning this relation is simply based on too narrow a conception of correspondence. Rorty seems to think of correspondence as representation or isomorphism. (CL 4, PDT 137.) But who needs that? Our beliefs neither share the structure of a world of states of affairs nor do they mirror the way the world is. Correspondence does not have to be conceived of as congruence but can equally well be conceived of as a correlation between our beliefs and ways the world is.[7]

6   Moreover, if Rorty were willing to accept an externalism about mental content, then why would he even set out to show skepticism pointless? Since externalism, if true, would suffice to refute skepticism, shouldn't he rather try to make a good case for externalism.

7   A word about correspondence as correlation: A sentence »p« uttered in a certain context is correlated to a way the world might be, namely p. If p obtains, »p« corresponds to the way the world is. If p does not obtain, »p« does not correspond to the way the world is. To give an example let us consider the following situation: In the morning Peter asks his dad whether the bathroom is occupied. His dad says »No, the bathroom is not occupied«. Uttering these words Peter *expects* the bathroom to be free. And Peter has this expectation because his dad's utterance is correlated to a possible way the world might be: namely, that the bathroom is free. Now, if the bathroom is really free the sentence Peter's dad uttered corresponds to the world. If it is occupied and Peter's brother is still taking a shower, the sentence does not cor-

4

In his critique against Cartesian skepticism, Rorty does not restrict himself to a rejection of tertia and the notion of correspondence alone, but tries to get rid of the fact-side of the relation as well. His aim is obvious: If he could demonstrate that there is nothing for our beliefs to correspond to, then the skeptical question how we can be sure that our beliefs correspond to the world becomes pointless.

Rorty does not deny the existence of an outside world. Although it is very hard to locate him exactly in this debate (for he thinks that as a pragmatist he stands beyond the realist-antirealist distinction[8]), he identifies himself as a realist at least in a very weak sense of the word when he asserts, »with common sense, that most things in space and time are the effects of causes which do not include human mental states.« (CL 5.)

It is just that he doesn't appreciate certain aspects of the way the world is conceived traditionally. His argument is two-pronged: First, Rorty doubts that it makes sense to think of our beliefs as being more or less closely in touch with the world. (CL 7.) This might best be expressed by his notorious thesis that »there is no Way the World Is«. (ITGI 25.) Secondly, according to Rorty, correspondence has to be conceived of as correspondence to facts. But we do not have any clear idea of what kind of entities the alleged facts could possibly be.

Let us turn to the first point. For Rorty, the world cannot function as a norm for our beliefs since it has no intrinsic nature or essence. (CL 4, 8, 21.) Therefore one cannot say that one language describes the world more adequately than another. The world is simply indifferent to our descriptions of

respond to the world. How the correlation between sentences uttered in contexts and ways the world might be is realized is a question psycho-linguists have to cope with. When we grow up, we just learn how sentences uttered in contexts are correlated to ways the world might be. But neither the signs »The bathroom is free« nor the respective sequence of sounds when you utter the sentence do resemble the world or share a structure with the world.

8   See for example the last of the four pragmatic theses about the nature of truth in PDT 128.

it. At least when we look at language games as a whole, no criteria of adequacy would be available. (CL 5.) Rorty proposes that we should *not* think of different language games as epistemic faculties which are made in order to represent the world in an accurate way, but rather as »tools for dealing with the world for one or another purpose.« (CL 21.) Rorty suggests that it is better to give up the idea of the world as an arbiter. In all cases only man-made, history-dependent conventional rules determine what we are justified to believe. For two reasons, this line of reasoning does not convince us.

First of all, following Rorty, new language games constantly introduce new purposes into our world. (CL 8, 12.) Why should the fulfillment of these human purposes not count as a criterion? Surely most physical theories serve the purpose of making exact predictions about nature. In order to achieve this goal they must apply the same criteria and the only way left to decide which theory best fulfills the criteria is by reliance on our experience of nature, our experience of the world.[9] And Rorty agrees that Newton's vocabulary lets us predict the world more accurately and more easily than Aristotle. (CL 6.) So given the same or at least translatable criteria, the world is no longer indifferent to competing theories.

Secondly, it is a platitude that our conventional rules change and that they play an important role in our way of justifying our beliefs. But it should also be clear that not all possible rules are equally appropriate for our purpose and that the world shows a kind of resistance. For instance, we could decide to call a closed door »open« in future; but it would make no difference to the door. We would still not be able to pass through it. Therefore, metaphorically speaking, the world plays its part as arbiter in our practice of accepting or dismissing certain beliefs.

So much for Rorty's first critique. Let us now turn to Rorty's arguments against facts. In his more recent paper »Is Truth a Goal of Inquiry?« (ITGI), Rorty argues against the conception of facts as sentence-shaped non-sentences which could serve as truth-makers. He writes: »insofar as they are non-conceptualized, they are not isolable as input. But insofar as they are conceptualized, they have been tailored to the needs of a particular input-output

---

9   Rorty at least does not explicitly deny the idea that, given the same criteria, only the
     world could decide between dissimilar theories. See his example of the verification
     of hypotheses in a given theory in CL 5.

function, a particular convention of representation.« (ITGI 36.) Thus all we can ever get are already conceptualized items. There are no world-made facts which can function as truth-makers.

But the skeptic has no need for such entities anyway. From the skeptic's standpoint, it makes no difference whether a little fraction of the world which is called a »fact« or whether the world as a whole makes a sentence true. For her purpose it is enough to give examples like the door example above to shift the burden of proof. More to the point, every further examination can not be in the skeptic's interest, because if she in fact finds a way to specify the facts, there would be no more room for raising her doubts.

So far, Rorty's theoretical doubts concerning the notion of correspondence are not convincing. Let us now turn to his pragmatist reservations.

5

According to Rorty, pragmatists think that »if something makes no difference to practice it should make no difference to philosophy.« (ITGI 19.) So, is the skeptic's claim just vacuous? Could it be that whether our beliefs do or do not correspond to an ontologically realistic world does not make any difference to our practice?

Rorty urges that the search for objective truth should not be seen as a search for correspondence, but instead as a search for the widest possible intersubjective agreement.[10] Search for the one and search for the other are the same kind of activity.[11] So an investigation into truth as correspondence becomes superfluous. The following objection comes quickly to mind:

It can hardly be denied that the search for truth and the search for intersubjective agreement are two different *goals* of human inquiry: Take two meteorologists – Paul and Carl – who work at a research facility for the prediction of long-term change in climate. Paul primarily intends to do his duty. In

---

10   SRR 63. To maintain, as Davidson does, that belief is in its nature veridical, is, according to Rorty, »not to celebrate the happy congruence of subject and object [respectively of tertia and reality] but rather to say that the pattern truth makes is the pattern that *justification to us* makes.« (ITGI 25.)

11   ITGI 19. Rorty is talking about truth as opposed to justification. His argument would stay the same if one replaces »truth« by »correspondence«.

order to make predictions he complies with the intersubjectively shared criteria of the present scientific community. His major concern is not to be subject to blame and reproach. The second researcher, Carl, primarily intends to make *true* predictions – predictions about what the world is going to be like. His major concern is that future generations will not suffer from the consequences of false predictions. Therefore, presumably the reactions of Paul and Carl would be quite different, if after a couple of years, through no fault of their own, their predictions will prove wrong.

Do Paul and Carl engage in the same kind of activity as Rorty is forced to claim? For two reasons we do not think so. First, Paul will do his work according to the regulations, while Carl will probably make supererogatory efforts to achieve his aim. Secondly, and more importantly, Paul will always try to comply with the standards accepted by present-day science, while Carl will also be looking for new ways of seeing things. It might even be the case that Carl manages to develop a revolutionary new and better theory. However, according to the currently shared standards of good climate research, such a theory would be unwarranted.

If the only goal of science were to maximize intersubjective agreement, it would be very hard to explain how new ideas heavily criticized by the scientific establishment could emerge as an integral part of science itself.[12]

Now let the skeptic insist that we do not have any knowledge of an external world. Rorty's answer is that knowledge is not a sensible topic of philosophy. But this answer *cannot* be based on the claim that whether we search for knowledge as opposed to justification makes no difference to our practice and thus no difference at all. (AW 163.)

Rorty concedes that pursuing truth – or correspondence for that matter – as distinct from intersubjective agreement is a different goal, but insists that the first goal is only of interest for metaphysically active inquirers who engage in metaphysics. (ITGI 29.) However, just someone's not being content with

---

12   For Rorty »great scientists invent descriptions of the world which are useful for purposes of predicting and controlling what happens, just as poets and political thinkers invent other descriptions of it for other purposes.« (CL 4.) But great scientists, if they *invent* descriptions at all, do not do so, because they want to be better justified according to contemporary scientific standards or even because they want to make a contribution to poetry! Their aim lies in developing theories whose predictions better fit with reality.

an intersubjective agreement does not mean that he is in a metaphysical frame of mind. Instead, he might be just struggling for a better understanding of our world, for a better fit of scientific predictions with reality, as it was the case with Darwin or Einstein.

Admittedly, the fact that, with respect to our motives for action, *distinguishing* internal justification from fitting with reality plays an important role, does neither show that there really is such a *difference*, nor that the skeptic is right in presupposing it. However, we have been trying to make clear, that the difference in question at least cannot be leveled or relativized with reference to pragmatism – quite the opposite!

But Rorty's notion of pragmatism might be wider than we have assumed. For example, Rorty seems to recommend the alleged »pragmatist habit of refusing to recognize the existence of trouble-making entities« (ITGI 20, note 4.) and prophesies that by the »substitution of self-creation for discovery« humanity will approach »closer and closer to the light.« (CL 20.)

From our point of view, it is not only difficult to see such a rhetoric as something like the expression of a pragmatist conviction, it is even hard to see such statements as expressing any sensible philosophical attitude at all. To recommend not paying attention to trouble-making entities on our way to the light is not a sensible rule in philosophy in just the same way, as to recommend ignoring annoying bacteria or viruses on our way to a long and sound life, is not a sensible rule in medicine.

6

Let us briefly sum up: Rorty wants to reject the skeptic instead of directly answering him, by demonstrating (a) that the skeptic needs a correspondence theory of truth and (b) that such a theory is implausible. We have granted that the skeptic at least needs a substantial notion of correspondence to make her point, but we have also argued that this notion is unproblematic given her needs and that Rorty's pragmatist reservations concerning this notion are unfounded.

In particular, we have first tried to show that (a) the sort of tertia the skeptic must assert is neither superfluous nor incompatible with a modern scientific approach nor dubious, (b) that the skeptic is not bound to rely on the conception of correspondence as representation and that (c) the skeptic does not have to assume the existence of so called facts, but can rely on the unproblematic assumption that the world plays an important role for the question as to which beliefs we should hold or dismiss.

Secondly, it does make a difference to practice whether we search for correspondence or for intersubjective agreement. We are therefore in the position to conclude that we have enough reason to doubt in good skeptical tradition the reality of an outside world and the plausibility of Rorty's arguments against Cartesian skepticism altogether.

REFERENCE

Kirkham, Richard L. 1992. *Theories of Truth – A Critical Introduction*, Cambridge, MA: MIT Press.

STRONG AND WEAK
METAPHYSICAL QUIETISM

*Stefan Heßbrüggen, Julia Heße, Rudolf Owen Müllan,
Stefan Reins, Ulrike Schuster, and Markus Seidel*

ABSTRACT: This paper is concerned with Rorty's attitude towards the conception of truth construed as an interesting metaphysical notion. In order to set his position off against other ones, Rorty draws an analogy between positions concerning this notion of truth and religious convictions. In this sense he compares his position – ›metaphysical quietism‹ – with atheism. However, sticking to this analogy we suggest that this metaphysical quietism is better understood as ›agnosticism,‹ which would also be coherent with the rest of Rorty's philosophy. The essay is concerned with reconstructing arguments for both positions leading to the question which one is to be preferred.

KEYWORDS: truth, atheism, agnosticism, metaphysical quietism

The Oxford English Dictionary defines quietism as »a state of calmness and passivity of mind or body.«[1] Rorty articulates in numerous passages of his oeuvre a view on truth, which he himself dubs ›metaphysical quietism.‹ (ITGI 29.) This seems to imply that the concept of truth is a metaphysical concept and that metaphysical concepts in general should not be able to disturb our peace of mind. The appropriate attitude to take is one of ›calmness and passivity of mind.‹

In our view, this position can be interpreted in two different ways, which we want to clarify by using an analogy proposed by Rorty himself. He compares metaphysical quietism to atheism: In the same way as atheists deny God's existence, a metaphysical quietist denies that metaphysical concepts in general, and the concept of truth in particular, denote any particular object or property. Yet, we believe that another strand can be isolated in Rorty's overall view that may be called ›agnosticism‹ about truth (and maybe metaphysical concepts in general, but we are not sure about that). On this agnosticist view, theories of truth are neither true nor false, but simply irrelevant: We need not care whether the concept of truth refers to some object or property, because answers to that question do not make any difference.

In what follows, we will first further explore the analogy between metaphysical concepts like truth and concepts used to express religious convictions and attitudes. Then we will try to locate the positions outlined above in Rorty's text and try to show that they are incompatible.

Our analysis of metaphysical quietism will concentrate on the concept of truth, though one ought to bear in mind that the position is not limited to reflections on truth, but pertains rather to metaphysical concepts in general. Rorty calls the opposing view ›metaphysical activism.‹ (ITGI 41 f.) According to his reading of his adversaries, they proceed on the undisputed fact that ›the world is out there‹ and arrive at the conclusion that ›truth is out there.‹ (Cf. CIS 4-5.) This claim can either be read as the contention that the concept of truth refers to an object or property of objects. Or it may be read as saying that linguistic phenomena (e. g. utterances) are made true by corresponding pieces of the world. We will concentrate on the second view. The metaphysical activist sees »attaining truth as distinct from making justified statements.« (ITGI 29.) It is this intuition (that truth transcends justification) that urges the metaphysical activist to describe the relation between utterances and the world in terms of a correspondence that confronts sentences with reality. We only mention the fact that neither coherentist nor minimalist accounts of truth share this assumption.

For Rorty, such activism seems to be a futile endeavor. (Cf. CIS 8, ITGI 42.) He presses the well-known point that no sense can be made of the correspondence-relation stated by the activist. He compresses this view in the Davidsonian slogan »correspondence without confrontation.«[2] While the metaphysical activist tries to offer a theory of truth by explaining the relation between the allegedly disparate realms of the linguistic and the non-linguistic, the metaphysical quietist takes the concept of truth as primitive and not in need of analysis. (PDT 137, CIS 8.) He has reached a state of calm tranquillity. (Cf. CIS 8.)

---

2   Davidson 1986, p. 307 (quoted in PDT 126).

Now, why is metaphysical quietism a derivation of atheism? The notion of atheism comes into play as Rorty stresses a connection between activist positions like the correspondence theory of truth and religious convictions. The metaphysical activist worships the concept of truth as something out there like the faithful worshipped the Gods. This is due to the fact that metaphysical concepts in general can be regarded as »a legacy of an age in which the world was seen as the creation of a being who had a language of his own.« (CIS 5.) Rorty draws on analyses presented e. g. by philosophers like Hans Blumenberg who has shown the intimate connection between the idea of a divine being that planned and created the world and the idea that we can find the truth out there in this world. Any philosophically substantial notion of God has vanished from our respective vocabulary, while we have, at the same time, retained the notion of truth. Throughout history, different surrogates for this conception of God as the creator of a cognitively accessible world have been introduced, says Rorty: The enlightenment tried to substitute the love of God by the love of truth. The romantic movement replaced the love of truth by the love of our inner self. (Cf. CIS 22.) All these surrogates work in the same way. Metaphysical activists do not understand this continuity and are thus held captive by a world view Rorty seems to regard as ›reactionary.‹ (Cf. CIS 21, SO 33, ITGI 32.)

How are we supposed to deal with this situation? Rorty himself professes himself to be an atheist concerning God as well as all surrogates invented to replace him in order to guarantee our cognitive success. Still we believe, and this is the thesis we want to defend here, that agnosticism about metaphysical questions is as compatible with important tenets of his overall view: Yet, both views are mutually exclusive.

Rorty wants to put an end to this seemingly endless process of introducing metaphysical surrogates by maintaining to »worship nothing as a quasi divinity.« (CIS 22.) This »consistent atheism would prevent us from inventing God surrogates like Reason, Nature, CSP [conceptual system Peirce, the world view at an ideal end of inquiry], or a Matter of Fact about Warrant.« (PRM 54.) All these metaphysical notions oblige us to introduce abstract, non-spatial entities (or, as Rorty says, *tertia*) that are supposed to somehow relate the allegedly disparate realms of the linguistic and the non-linguistic in a non-causal way. (Cf. PDT 139.) Such entities mediate between our utterances and the world, and thus help to make sense of ›truth as correspondence to reality.‹ (Cf. PDT 138.) According to Rorty, however, Davidson has shown that such entities are superfluous. His theory of radical interpretation tells a purely causal story of the relation between beliefs and the environment. (Cf. PDT 128, 135, 139.) It has no need for such mediating entities, they »are just not there.« (PDT 138.) Now we can see why Rorty calls such a view atheist. Metaphysical concepts do not denote, their reference is empty.

But what is the motivation for such claims? We have discerned the following two lines of argument:

The argument from historical evidence: Following Dewey, Rorty argues that secularization has been a major driving force behind many social improvements that we today, from our point of view, would clearly describe as better. (RCD 197.) As examples of this development towards secularism he gives us »Socrates' turn away from the gods, Christianity's turn from an Omnipotent Creator to the man who suffered on the Cross, and the Baconian turn from science as contemplation of eternal truth to science as instrument of social progress.« (SO 33.) Since such demystification of the world has lead to an enhancement of our cultural as well as social environment, it might be a good idea to demolish the last remainders of a non-secular world view. Of course, the force of Rorty's argument rests on the assumption that the development he describes really is welcomed in principle by everyone, at least by the inhabitants of the modern secular West.

The argument from Darwinism: Darwinism is a way of understanding our own species, which is particularly compatible with quietism, because it does not require us to fall back on metaphysical posits. We no longer need to point to an intrinsic human nature in order to explain our specific abilities, but can construe them as complex adaptations. But evolution is not teleological, since mutated genes survive accidentally through their better adaptation to their environment. With Dawkins' theory of Memes in the background (RCD 191), we may pretty much say the same of cultural evolution. If there is no telos, we are forced to reject the idea of us »as heading towards a place which has somehow been prepared for humanity in advance.« (SO 28.) Quite to the contrary, it actually seems far more plausible that our culture and, with it, our norms are constantly changing, thus making our justifications highly contingent – which does not leave any space for a justification-transcendent notion of truth. (Cf. HSE 35.)

Rorty draws the conclusion that we should play a new, consistently atheist language game in the hope that it will prevail over our actual one. The suggestion is that, with »Nietzschean history of culture, and Davidsonian philosophy of language,« we should come to »see language as we now see evolution, as new forms of life constantly killing off old forms – not to accomplish a higher purpose, but blindly.« (CIS 19.) Even if we do not know what the future will look like, Rorty has the strong conviction that an atheist language game will be the appropriate way to attain this goal.

In order to identify the weaknesses of these arguments directly, we now propose a different view of the problem of truth, which can be reconstructed from several hints in Rorty's writings. To us, it is compatible with Rorty's overall philosophical convictions, and may avoid some of the problems of the atheist view. We call it ›metaphysical agnosticism.‹

Rorty's main motivation for giving up the concept of truth does not seem to be some kind of ›ontological conviction‹ but ›merely‹ the practical reason that he considers a treatment of this concept an »unprofitable topic« (CIS 8.) – too troublesome to cope with it any longer. This, we think, makes it questionable whether he really is committed to his explicitly stated strong claim that there *is* no such thing like truth in the above mentioned sense. (CIS 5-6, 7, 20-21, PDT 132, 138.)

Our criticism of an atheist view of metaphysical notions rests mainly on four points:

– The atheist's claim is too strong.
– It is not compatible with his own meta-philosophical premises.
– It is not compatible with the Davidsonian holism accepted by Rorty.
– It only rests on a contingent claim of what may be regarded as ›better‹ by future generations.

If Rorty wants to stop what he regards as endless and fruitless attempts to find an adequate philosophical analysis of truth – as well as related concepts – and to replace this by »new and possibly interesting questions,« (CIS 9) the claim that the concept is empty seems to be too strong. It would be sufficient just to give up talking about it, to be an ›agnosticist‹ about this point. And, indeed, this is exactly what Rorty concedes himself, when he says that it would be sufficient for his purposes just to stop bothering about the term ›truth,‹[3] »which has caused more trouble than it has been worth.« (CIS 8, SO 33.)

According to Rorty, the way we think about the world and ourselves depends on the vocabularies we use.[4] So any change in our vocabularies induces changes in our beliefs and habits. To replace the notion of truth and the associated metaphysical vocabulary by more interesting paradigms and vocabularies should in itself be sufficient to make the notion irrelevant. Since any discussion about what makes up ›real‹ truth, the ›correct‹ language game which represents the world perfectly, is impossible, there is no way he can ›argue‹ for his position in the strict sense; all he can do is try to show that talking in a different way would be ›better‹ for us.[5] For that, it is neither necessary nor even possible to prove that the atheist is right.

Finally, we should bear in mind that Davidson's holism does not allow us to find out exactly which of our beliefs are true – a conviction which is shared by Rorty.[6] Why should that not be the case for metaphysical beliefs? The agnosticist avoids this problem.

Still, agnosticism shares some problems with the atheist view. We will conclude our paper by articulating some fundamental doubts about Rorty's philosophical project. In his argument from historical evidence, Rorty expresses the hope that a thorough secularization of our vocabularies may make the world a better place. But for Rorty, these improvements can only be assessed from a *post festum* perspective, that is, *after* the language game has already changed and therefore enabling us to compare the new language game which we are in with the older one. (SO 29, CIS 9.) But, nevertheless, Rorty anticipates the new situation and hopes that, by changing the present situation according to his suggestions, our grandchildren may have the conviction that

3   »Truth« in this context is understood in the sense of »intrinsic nature« (CIS 8).
4   »It is changing the way we talk, and thereby changing what we want to do and what we think we are « (CIS 20).
5   »The difficulty faced by a philosopher who, like myself, is sympathetic to this suggestion – one who thinks of himself as auxiliary to the poet rather than to the physicist – is to avoid hinting that this suggestion gets something right, that my sort of philosophy corresponds to the way things really are« (CIS 7-8).
6   »We shall never know for sure whether a given belief is true [...]« (UT 2).

the world has changed to the better. So, though an adequate comparison can only be made after the change has been completed, Rorty, of course, already *now* judges his vision as ›better‹ with respect to the situation we live in – by envisioning a version of »*us* at our best.«[7]

The *hope* for a better future indeed is the only ›argument‹ for his pragmatist position. He himself emphasizes that, if we shared his vision and followed him, hope would not be enough, for we would need *luck* also.[8]

Originally, quietism was »a form of religious mysticism (originated prior to 1675 by Molinos, a Spanish priest), consisting in passive devotional contemplation, with extinction of the will and withdrawal from all things of the senses.«[9] Of course this is not what Rorty proposes. But since the pragmatist has only the contemporary, representationalist picture and its, for Rorty, ›unfortunate‹ (TTGI 41) vocabulary at hand in order to put forward her own picture of truth and justification, and, in this sense, cannot step out of her cultural fixation at the cost of self-contradiction, she »is in the same situation as are atheists in overwhelmingly religious cultures.« (Cf. ibid.) In her position she cannot claim to have found out the truth about ›truth,‹ but to believe in just

7   PRM 52, see also p. 54: »When we picture a better version of ourselves, we build into this picture the evolution of this better version out of our present selves through a process in which actualizations of these values played an appropriate part.« Cf. also HSE 17: »[B]esser insofern, als mehr unserer Meinung nach Gutes und weniger unserer Meinung nach Schlechtes darin enthalten ist.«

8   Cf. HSE 15-16: »Sofern der Pragmatismus überhaupt etwas Spezifisches an sich hat, dann dies: Daß er die Begriffe der Realität, der Vernunft und des Wesens durch den Begriff der besseren menschlichen Zukunft ersetzt.« See also p. 20 (»die Gegenwart sei ein Übergangsstadium auf dem Weg zu etwas, das unvorstellbar viel besser sein könne, falls wir Glück haben«), 25 (»Die Forderung, man solle die Erkenntnis durch Hoffnung ersetzen, besagt im großen und ganzen das gleiche: Man sollte sich nicht mehr darum kümmern, ob das, was man glaubt, gut fundiert ist, sondern sich allmählich darum kümmern, ob man genügend Phantasie aufgebracht hat, um sich interessante Alternativen zu den gegenwärtigen Überzeugungen auszudenken«) and 34: »Da niemand die Zukunft kennt, weiß auch niemand, welche Überzeugungen ihre Berechtigung behalten und welche nicht; und daher gibt es nichts Ahistorisches, was sich über die Erkenntnis oder die Wahrheit sagen ließe. Daß man nichts weiter sagt, hat den Effekt, daß das, was Europa der Metaphysik und der Erkenntnistheorie überantwortet hat, an die Hoffnung übergeht. Es hat den Effekt, daß man Platons Versuch, der Zeit zu entrinnen, durch die Hoffnung ersetzt, wir könnten eine bessere Zukunft hervorbringen.«

9   OED, vol. 13, p. 26.

another kind of religion that tries to survive in cultural evolution. (HSE 35.) Thus pragmatism is something like ›the specific American religion.‹ (Cf. HSE 32.)

Adherents of this particular creed share the belief in a future where all people are, like Rorty, »liberal ironists,« »western liberal intellectuals« – people who hold to their language and convictions though they know that these are contingent and are no better suited to reality than others. Rorty wants us to become »the people who are always willing to hear the other side, to think out all the implications, and so on.« (PRM 52.) But if this is the main goal he aims at, one can wonder, with Putnam, about the way Rorty proposes to us for achieving this aim: »If your aim is tolerance and the open society, would it not be better to argue for these directly, rather than to hope that these will come as the by-product of a change in our metaphysical picture?« (PRM 58.) Indeed, Rorty concedes that he does not take the way proposed by him as the only possible or the most advisable one to get to Utopia. At least, in a passage taken from *Hinter den Spiegeln*, he writes that he would be happy if we could extend our »Wir-Gefühl« by means of transcendental arguments à la Habermas, but in case this should not work, we could still try further methods.[10]

The main points of our paper can be summarized in the following questions:

– Is it the case that both interpretations are mutually exclusive? If not, how are they related?
– If they are mutually exclusive, does Rorty agree that metaphysical agnosticism is to be preferred?

---

10 »Falls es mit Hilfe transzendentaler Argumente à la Habermas wirklich gelingen sollte, das Wir-Gefühl zu erweitern, fände ich das prima. Falls es nicht klappt, gibt es ja noch weitere Verfahren, mit denen wir es probieren können« (ETS 198).

REFERENCES

Davidson, Donald 1986. »A Coherence Theory of Truth and Knowledge,« in: *Truth and Interpretation, Perspectives on the Philosophy of Donald Davidson*, ed. by Ernest Le Pore, Oxford: Blackwell, p. 307-319.

–, 2000. »Truth Rehabilitated«, in: *Rorty and His Critics*, ed. by Robert B. Brandom, Oxford: Blackwell, p. 65-74.

OED. *The Oxford English Dictionary*, Second Edition, prepared by J. A. Simpson and E. S. C. Weiner, Oxford: Clarendon Press, 1989.

THE WORLD REGAINED?

Ludwig Siep

ABSTRACT: Richard Rorty rejects the idea of a world »behind« our views of things. On his view, there is no essence and no true nature which might function in discourse as an external corrective to subjective attitudes (concepts, theories, valuations etc.). Therefore he recommends to conceptually get rid of the world. This paper argues that there is room for regaining the world without restoring traditional philosophical or ethical dualisms in the tradition of Plato or Kant. By means of a holistic conception of goodness and a relational theory of values the idea of a »good world« may be reestablished. It can serve as a criterion for our technological and legal options concerning the variety and flourishing of natural beings as well as human cultures and individual rights.

KEYWORDS: world, cosmos, concept of nature, essentialism, ontological holism, natural flourishing

Richard Rorty does not like »the world«. He thinks we should be happy to loose it – that is, we should not talk about the world as something behind our views of things, events, situations etc.[1] Just as things have no essence beyond their relation to each other and to our perception and understanding, there is no essence or true nature of the world beyond our descriptions and theories about it. Consequently the world is not what makes our statements about these objects true or false. Instead, what makes theories or stories about such objects true or otherwise valuable is their efficiency in explaining data, control or predict events and contribute to a good human life. Even particle physics should not grasp at true explanations but contribute to technological progress and create new descriptions of the universe as a whole (HSE 53).

By contrast, I myself have argued, that ethics should regain the world. (Cf. Siep 2004.) Instead of asking only for duties towards human beings, we should ask again what would fit in a possible »cosmos«, a world which can be called »good« in the sense of being universally approvable and worth to be strived for. World-wide conventions about the preservation of the diversity of

---

1   Cf. his famous paper »The World Well Lost« (WWL).

species and landscapes, about sustainable development, cultural pluralism and the protection of human rights in a comprehensive sense require such a background vision of a good world to which human beings may contribute or which they may hinder.

Are we talking about the same »world«? I suspect not. In what follows, I try to specify in which way I agree with Richard Rorty's deconstruction of »the world« and why I still think that we need this concept – especially where we have lost it in modern times, namely in ethics.

1

My agreement with Rorty concerns his skepticism against the traditional dualisms of philosophy and against all forms of »absolutes« in the form of beings (entia necessaria), truths or practical principles to which every possible alternative would be self-contradictory. Concerning the »map« of the human mental faculties I share his doubts about a clear distinction between reason and »the rest«, namely emotions, sense perceptions etc.[2] I also agree with him that there is no way to ever prove that our descriptions and explanations of the world are final and not open to further corrections or »scientific revolutions«. And concerning ethics I agree that there are no final principles or »truths« to justify our values, norms and duties – neither in the world, nor in practical reason, intersubjectivity or a process of rational communication. What remains both in science and in ethics or law is a process of experiences with values and norms which tells us what to our present knowledge are the right norms and values.[3]

On the other hand, together with some of Rorty's critics I doubt that along with the idea of an absolute world, which may be different from everything we believe about things, events etc., we have to give up the idea of some sort of response of an independent reality in scientific as well as moral and legal experiences. Therefore I firstly opt for a mix of coherence and correspondence theory of truth. And secondly I am not convinced of the exclus-

2   Cf. Siep 2004, p. 177 f., where I argue for a holistic concept of reason. Also my »Vernunft und Tugend« (forthcoming as Siep 2005).
3   I have argued for this position in Siep 2004, p. 34 f., 54 f., 164 f.

iveness of Rorty's criteria for scientific and moral progress, namely utility and imagination regarding theoretical knowledge and solidarity regarding practical values, norms and institutions.

As to the first point, »weak« realism concerning scientific and moral/legal experiences, Kompa et al. in this volume have given plausible arguments concerning the »resistance« of something outside our language and theory formation against rules and hypotheses (cf. 79 f.). Against a widespread projectivism in value theory I would argue that the same is true for many of our value expressions such as »healthy«, »to be feared«, even »valuable« and – if to a less controversial degree – »good«. As there is no »prima materia« or »given« completely outside our theoretical concepts, there is no completely neutral material for our value concepts either.

It is some property of the food, not just our way of seeing it, describing it or valuing it, which makes it healthy, dangerous etc. We can fail if we confront things, persons and events with wrong descriptions, expectations and evaluations. Many values and valuable experiences are discovered by surprise either individually or collectively. This sort of discovery in exchange with a »resistant reality« occurs also concerning ethical values like friendship or new forms of justice and charity. And moral or legal »solutions« of problems are exposed to confirmation or refutation by future events and experiences similar to technical solutions or scientific hypotheses. There may be more controversy about the interpretation of these experiences and their lessons – but this seems to me a matter of degree, not of principle.

I cannot go into the details of the debate about the ontological and epistemological status of values here, for instance the question whether values are secondary qualities. There are analogies but also important differences between values and colors or noises. But the whole conception of primary and secondary qualities seems to be tied to the idea of »fixed« subjects and objects with properties either »in themselves« or in mutual interaction. However, our statements about properties always seem to be grounded in interactions with our environment. It is doubtful that we can ever get to properties like Lockean primary qualities which objects possess only for themselves, without any relation to human attitudes.[4]

---

4   This is not to say that in the process of science we cannot overcome a lot of subjective and anthropomorphic perspectives – as Thomas Nagel claims in »The View from

The same seems to hold for the subjective side: the formation of wishes and interests cannot be separated from our theoretical and practical interaction with states of affairs, persons, things etc. which turn out to be valuable, worthless or detrimental. Of course, individual valuations may trace back to cultural values and habits formed by a long tradition. But their sources are again individual and collective experiences with reactions by something not constituted by our wishes and expectations – both inside and outside the acting, perceiving and theorizing human being.

In defending such a weak realism – which I can only sketch here[5] – I do not consider myself very far apart from Rorty's position. I am not a »true believer« in some ultimate reality beyond our reflected and scientifically corroborated statements. As to moral and legal norms, I suspect that their justification lies in a mixture of enduring and resistant collective experiences – shared by ever larger communities – on the one hand and theories about why something is good or bad for mankind and its different groups and individuals on the other. Such theories are worked out by different sciences, among them anthropology and philosophy. They can never be final in the sense of being without a self-contradictory alternative – although it seems very unlikely that mankind may ever come up with convincing reasons connected with broadly shared experiences for, say, reintroducing slavery or gender discrimination.

My second deviation from Rorty concerns his criteria for progress both with regard to scientific theories and moral experiences.

I am not convinced that imagination and technical applicability or control and prediction are the only criteria to distinguish between good or bad scientific theories. As to imagination or new ways of seeing the world, I agree that enlarging our horizon and looking at the world from new perspectives is one of the most important criteria for spiritual progress. But as to scientific explanations of natural beings, events and processes, and even some elementary layer of historical facts, there seem to be methodical requirements which set limits to scientific imagination. Against »constructivism« both regarding the natural and the historical sciences I think that by scientific experiments and methods like excavations and the study of inscriptions and documents we

Nowhere« (Nagel 1986).
5   For more details cf. Siep 2004, p. 135 ff.

can correct our hypotheses or historical »stories« by some sort of »answer« provided by things and processes in the world. By applying such methods we can arrive at more appropriate descriptions and functional explanations than the ones we had before.[6]

In an analogous way I am inclined to think that our experiences with social norms and institutions can get closer to what is appropriate for human beings and even to the non-human objects and partners. For normal human beings – maybe except for great ascetics or artists who creatively exploit their sufferings or extreme situations – it is more appropriate to get healthy food, not to be tortured or oppressed by slaveholders, not to be discriminated because of race or gender etc. Although mankind has very likely discovered these »truths« and the corresponding norms and institutions in its cultural history, they can be called appropriate to human faculties, the conditions of a good life and in this weak sense to the human »essence«. Therefore we can distinguish, even if not in an absolute way, between changes of values and institutions on the one hand and »barbarizations« or destructions of human institutions on the other.

I am in sympathy with Rorty's idea of a progress of compassion and solidarity starting with the family and comprising ever wider circles of human beings. But I am skeptical whether this is enough to justify what is good and bad in human behavior and what can count as progress to a better future. It seems that Rorty parallels the growing amount of data we have to explain through a plausible and coherent theory in the sciences on the one hand and the concern for a growing number of human beings on the other. (Cf. HSE 79 ff.) But it is well known that concern or sympathy is not always the best source and motivation of appropriate behavior against human and other beings.[7] And why should we enlarge our solidarity as much as possible, if this is not what human beings beyond our group deserve?

What we owe to each other – to quote Thomas Scanlon's title – does not completely depend on our benevolent feelings but on what is good for the

6   I am not convinced that these methods can be reduced to the activities of control and prediction. Even in some fields of the natural sciences like geography or morphology – think of Nabokov's butterflies – there are other ways of describing and explaining how things function, how they are composed and what are their different shapes and faculties.

7   Think of paternalism, overprotectiveness or Böll's »fürsorgliche Belagerung«.

other.[8] And in order to qualify a behavior as good if it satisfies other peoples needs, demands or claims we need a basic idea of what is good – namely what contributes to a state of affairs which is universally[9] approvable and worth to be strived for. I think that even Rorty's »summum malum«, namely cruelty in the form of physical and psychical sadism – breaking another's personality – needs some explanation of what is hurt both in the subject and the objects of such actions.[10]

In my view, this does not mean to go back to something absolute, a last principle of goodness or an unconditional good like the Kantian good will.[11] It suffices to go back to the development of views about what is good in human society and in the world in general. Values, which I consider to be the sources of norms, do not belong to an ideal or purely intelligible world. They are founded in descriptions and experiences of valuable aspects of things, actions, events, states of affairs etc. And in the same way in which Rorty still talks about »the universe« as the comprehensive explanandum of the natural sciences one can speak of »a good world« both as the comprehensive framework of criteria for good behavior and intentions – which have to fit in such a world – and as the bearer of the valuable aspects and properties which we refer to in moral or »all things considered« value-judgments.

2

Whereas I argue that in a secularized and post-metaphysical way we should revive the old concepts of a good world as cosmos or creation – not in the

8   Cf. T. Scanlon 1999. I would argue against Scanlon, however, that experiences of what is good or valuable for human beings determine the reasons for their claims and our responses – not the other way around (cf. Siep 2004, p. 182).
9   »Universally« not in the sense that pure reason in every human person must necessarily approve, but that everybody who shares our moral language and our value experiences has convincing reasons to approve – »our« referring to at least the European tradition but aiming at enlarging its horizon into an intercultural consensus (at least an »overlapping« consensus in Rawls' sense).
10   Cf. CIS 169 ff.
11   This does not exclude unconditionally wrong intentions (like the intention to do the bad for its own sake or for the pleasure it gives) or actions (like those rendering a good world impossible).

sense of a causal product with an eternal form but as a possible temporary state of the evolutionary process – Richard Rorty attacks precisely the Greek and Christian concepts of an absolute and optimal world order. Isn't that an insurmountable gulf between our positions?

Surely, in the traditional versions of cosmos and creation the meaning was exactly that of a necessary and ideal order stemming from a perfectly rational, benevolent and omnipotent reason and will. Whether it was attainable by human reason and striving or not, whether it could be known or fulfilled at all or to which degree, varies according to the different philosophical and theological positions in our tradition. In the modern age, this perfect world seems to have lost its magic (»entzaubert«), but its epistemological and normative function has been taken over by »the subject« or »the rational discourse«. Therefore, ethics is no more concerned with a good world but with an unconditionally good will or rationally justified norms of behavior between the only beings with a »moral status«, namely human beings.

Against these forms of foundationalism be it absolute realism, subjectivism or intersubjectivism, I have argued with Rorty that the history of science and ethics has to be regarded as a historical process of experiences and the formation of revisable theories, norms and institutions. Regarding ethics and law I think that mankind has gathered a store of such values, norms and institutions in a long history of (mostly painful) experiences.[12] And I also think that from the beginning of religion and morality human actions have been judged as »good« in the moral or »all things considered« sense if they contributed to or at least did not disturb or hinder a good state of affairs in the world they inhabited.[13] »World« in this sense did not always mean a final reality but

12   In this view I am, of course, influenced by Hegel's conception of the »Arbeit des Weltgeistes«. But I do not think that Hegel's conception of an absolute completion of this work can still be defended. There are, however, interpretations of Hegel's term »absolute« like for instance Terry Pinkard's, who understand absolute spirit and absolute knowledge as the permanent cultural discourse which overturns every claim to absolute validity. Concerning the debate on Hegel's understanding of the term »absolute« cf. Pinkard's, Steckeler-Weithofer's, Fulda's and my contributions to Halbig, Quante, Siep 2005.

13   The ethical meaning of the religious concept of a life pleasing to God or a veneration of God in his creation is the demand to contribute to the good state of the world. In many ancient religions the right veneration of the gods (in cult and daily life) is not only necessary for the welfare of individuals and groups but also for the

often just everything in the reach of human experience. In a time of coexist-
ence between religious and secular world-views it is this meaning which can
serve as a comprehensive criterion for right and wrong human behavior.

But why do we need the concept »world« in addition to the concepts of
things, events, persons, processes etc. and why a »good world« in addition to
good actions, good intentions, characters, states of affairs etc.? In my view,
because ethics tries to find out what is »truly« valuable and not just »prima
facie« or even in everybody's (including the murderer's) private perspective.
And if there are no absolute criteria for this truth, it is only on the basis of
our history of well-founded experiences that we can ask for the right conditions (intentions, dispositions, character) and the good consequences of actions and norms for a world approvable without restrictions. They are not to
be measured against some absolute criterion like »the pleasure-pain balance«[14]
but rather in a coherentist way: They have to fit together in a whole of valuable actions and states of affairs. The values which these actions »realize« are
again nothing absolute, independent, »Platonic«. They are rather abbreviations
of shared value experiences (which can sometimes be expressed in value-
judgments).[15] But these experiences are about something which can resist our
wishes and volitions and can reverse our expectations and prejudices – in this
sense they are about something in the world, comprising the experiencing being.

Thus the term »world« in the »good world« has a double meaning:
Firstly, that of an encompassing whole of persons, actions, consequences and
values which can be called »good« or »worth to be approved and strived for
by everybody«. Secondly, that this whole to which every action and value contributes is not something ideal, not a supernatural realm of ends or a heaven

preservation of the world order.

14   Like Richard Rorty (HSE 69 f.), I think that utilitarianism still uses an »absolute« cri-
       terion because it assumes that at the end of all days one could definitively decide
       about the »real« sums of pains and pleasures. For me, the goodness of the world is
       not something to be maximized – it is only a set of conditions (like diversity, justice,
       flourishing, welfare, interpersonal respect etc.) to be met. Of course, meeting them
       will mean producing or preserving a certain sum of states valuable under different
       perspectives.
15   In this respect I would argue for a contextualist concept of values: We can explain
       the meaning of »justice« only by referring to descriptions of types and finally particu-
       lar instances of just actions, distributions etc.

of ideal values (»Wertehimmel«) but simply the world we inhabit regarded in its valuable aspects. Some of these – as in the arts – may be (or may have been) »created« by human inventions, but even these must be affirmed by common experiences.[16] Some can only be derived or imagined by reflecting on our bad experiences. Of course, the valuable aspects of the social and natural world are not all realized as yet – nor might they be completely realized in any future state of affairs.[17] It is enough to ask whether an action or norm fits with what we have experienced or can expect with some reliability to belong to an overall good state of affairs.

The conception of a good world as extracted from the traditional religions and philosophies at least of the Western[18] world contains a few formal criteria which are connected to the very concept of a world as a structured and ordered whole different from nothingness or chaos.[19] However, they need not to be considered »conceptually necessary« or a priori. They have probably also been developed in cultural history. Among them are the concepts of a diversity of independent beings of different forms, types or species, of some balance between conflict and co-existence, and the conditions of such co-existence, namely some basic fair share of resources. And since »good« is what is worth for the parts and participants to strive for or approve, the flourishing and well being of at least those beings which are able to enjoy it belongs to a good world.[20]

16   As to invention or discovery of values, there seems to be a scale from one of these two extremes (invention and discovery) to the other according to the sort and sphere of values (art, nature, social life etc.).

17   Not because the good world is a »regulative idea« which is impossible to realize in the sensible world, but because, for all we know, human beings – at least in a biological constitution similar to the present one – will not stop to make new and unexpected value experiences.

18   To my knowledge, however, such a »cosmic« conception of the good seems to be at least equally familiar in other, especially Asian, cultures.

19   Of course, there are some »acosmic« religious and philosophical positions which consider the world to be irretrievably bad or corrupted. But they are of little significance for worldly ethics.

20   Such an idea of a »well-ordered cosmos« does not exclude the fighting of groups for the enlargement of their biological niche. But it should restrict the human technological optimization of nature – especially if this is guided only by private wishes and marketing opportunities.

Ludwig Siep

One may argue that at least the last two components of the concept of a good world – basic fairness or justice and flourishing or well-being – can vary between different cultural enrichments or elaborations of the formal concept of a good world. If so, they have at least a long history and a wide distribution in our religious and ethical traditions. And they seem to gain more and more global approval in recent times of intercultural normative consensus formation.

Traditional ethics has been based on a dualism between the rational and the non-rational – the former being of incomparable higher worth (or dignity) than the latter. Together with the foundationalist conceptions of dualisms in other fields of philosophy we should overcome this dualism too. That means to give up the exclusion of everything non-human from the claim of being treated in the right way. To be sure, only human beings can act morally, but not necessarily only against other human beings.

But even if we remain in the field of interpersonal norms, today we have to deal with many questions concerning the value of natural properties and processes. Contemporary bioethics deals with questions of conservation or improvement of the human genetic condition and of similar biotechnological options concerning non-human nature. Even if one considers, like Richard Rorty, the cultural self-creation of individuals to be among the most valuable goals of human activity, it is not certain that genetic improvement would serve that goal.[21] In my view, the questions of the worth and the permission for such far-reaching technical interventions can be judged only in view of what we have experienced as valuable or detrimental concerning the human constitution and the natural and cultural environment.[22]

If ethics is involved – certainly not as the only voice – in deliberating about technological options of such range, it has to consider consequences for all generations to come and to a great part of the cosmos. And this in the light of almost all we know about our past and of most of our scientific

---

21   It could, for instance, abolish the possibility to make unexpected experiences – after all, the control and avoidance of contingencies is an immanent aim of technology.

22   It would not do to restrict these forms of biological self-creation or self-improvement to the sphere of the private – as Rorty suggests regarding cultural self-perfection (CIS 33 f.), especially in view of radical self-images (CIS 197). Genetic enhancement, if feasible in the way imagined nowadays, would have far-reaching social consequences. Cf. Siep 2003 and 2004, 316 f.

knowledge. Even if its reflections take place in the context of a particular tradition and culture, they aim at overcoming these limitations and reach out for intercultural consensus. The guiding picture is that of a world with as much cultural and natural variety as we have inherited and as much human rights and flourishing, including meaningful common goals and individual self-realizations reconcilable without violent destructions and dominations. In the light of this encompassing idea and not only of individual rights and interests philosophical ethics as part of the public discussion can try to judge the promises and the costs of technological and political options as well as legal and economic developments. When I call that guiding idea and framework for ethical judgment a »good world«, it is certainly not meant as an absolute reality behind all – possibly erroneous – theories and evaluations.

In this sense, I think, at least ethics should regain the world – not the same world, it seems to me, as that which Rorty advises us to loose happily.

References

Halbig, Christoph, Michael Quante and Ludwig Siep 2005. *Hegels Erbe und die theoretische Philosophie der Gegenwart*, Frankfurt a. M.: Suhrkamp (forthcoming).

Nagel, Thomas 1986. *The View from Nowhere*, New York, Oxford: Oxford Univ. Pr.

Scanlon, Thomas 1999. *What We Owe to Each Other*, Cambridge, London: Cambridge Univ. Pr.

Siep, Ludwig 2004. *Konkrete Ethik*, Frankfurt: Suhrkamp.

Siep, Ludwig 2003. »Normative Aspects of the Human Body«, in: *The Journal of Medicine and Philosophy* 28, p. 171-185.

Siep, Ludwig 2005. »Vernunft und Tugend«, forthcoming in: *Abwägende Vernunft, Festschrift für Friedo Ricken*, ed. by. Franz-Josef Bormann and Christian Schröer.

COMMENTS AND RESPONSES

Richard Rorty

I am very grateful to the philosophy faculty at Münster for arranging my visit there, and to the students who produced the papers to which I respond below. The papers are of very high quality indeed, and the level of discussion during the day I spent with the students was equally high. I have never, in any university, encountered students who combined such detailed knowledge of my writings with such penetrating criticisms of my views. That combination made the day-long discussions very profitable for me, and the experience of writing out my responses has proved equally useful. It seems to me very remarkable that the Münster students were able to discuss philosophy in fluent English, and to wield the technical jargons used by various English-speaking philosophers with skill and finesse. The *Münstersche Vorlesungen zur Philosophie* series is an imaginative, and very successful, venture. It is a model of how to initiate students into a humanistic academic discipline. Philosophy departments around the world would do well to consider adopting this model.

Response to »Strong Poets, Privileged Self-Narratives, and ›We Liberals‹«

If there is a »tension between Rorty's espousal for growing diversity and recognition of mutual contingencies and his expressed commitment to solidarity«, surely this is because there is always a tension between freedom and organization. I do not see that I have more of a problem with the tension between diversity and solidarity than does any organizer of a labor union, or of an artistic movement, or of a political revolution. Anybody who tries to transform a collection of free citizens into a group whose members will submerge their individual differences in a common cause faces the same problem.

There can hardly be an interesting *general* answer to the question »how we are supposed to arrive at a collective ›we‹ rather than a multitude of individual voices«. The various authors of »Strong poets ...« presumably solved this problem *ambulando* when they created the text on which I am commenting. The Greens and the SPD solved it when they agreed on a coalition government. There as many different answers to that question as there are different sorts of group efforts.

To say that »everyone should have the same right to choose what heroes she wants to regard as exemplary« is like saying that everybody should have the same right to join whichever group she finds attractive. Of course. But what can any of us do save commend, and argue in favor of, the heroes we have found exemplary and the joint efforts we think worth joining? How could one have a general theory about how to pick the right heroes and heroines, or to decide which groups are worth joining? What would such a theory look like? What, in particular, would »criteria for adjudicating between conflicting traditions of – presumably good and bad liberalism« look like?

Any proposal for general criteria will be viewed by liberals belonging to the traditions of liberalism I dislike (e. g., communitarianism) as question-begging. It is a philosopher's myth that wherever there is a dispute there are neutral criteria available for resolving that dispute. We resolve lots of disputes without either applying neutral criteria or resorting to force; I would bet that Henning, Parthe, Rissing, Sieverding and Wenning resolved many disputes, without doing either, when they were working out what to say. Liberals resolve such disputes by reaching temporary ad hoc compromises in the same way that conservatives, and everyone else, do.

The idea that philosophical reflection might give us such neutral criteria is of a piece with the idea that there is a discipline called »critical theory« that can make a distinctive contribution to political struggles. Critical theory would be distinct from political rhetoric only if its practioners could locate some neutral standpoint which enabled them to distinguish people's *true* interests from »misleading pictures of who we are and what we do« that have been imposed by »the forces, interests and mechanisms inert in the social sphere«. But all that critical theorists have ever done, or ever can do, is to envisage a social utopia and then try to get people to describe themselves in ways that make that utopia seem attractive.

When people like me tell American evangelical Christians to vote their economic interests by voting Democratic we are, or should not, be saying »We know what your true interests are better than you do«. Rather, we are saying »Think of yourself as someone entitled to a share of the social product rather than as someone with a personal relation to Jesus, a divinity who can be relied upon to look after your welfare«. It does not take anything as sophisticated as »critical theory« or »the hermenutics of suspicion« to formulate the distinction between these two possible self-images.

Debate between alternative social utopias (the one envisaged by the fundamentalist Christians in Texas as much as the one envisaged by the Greens in Germany) is, among other things, a debate about who we are and what we do. But critical theorists are in no better a position to know who we *really* are and what we *really* do than are the people whom they accuse of »false consciousness«. All that either the fundamentalist or the Greens can do, in a democratic society, is to propose alternative self-descriptions to their fellow-citizens, and to denounce those proposed by their rivals as »distorted by underlying mechanisms of the social macrostructure«. Proposing such alternatives, and making such accusations, has always has been a useful form of political rhetoric. But I do not think that people trained in philosophy are better at deploying such rhetoric than other people.

I entirely agree that it »takes considerable amounts of leisure and financial as well as symbolic capital to make up an authentic identity by narration«. Nobody doubts that »the quest for unique ways of self-articulation is not among the prior problems an average construction worker has to cope with«. But the social democratic dream is that any construction worker who happens to be interested in unique ways of self-articulation will be as able to pursue that interest as are lawyers, accountants and philosophy professors, because he or she will have the same amount of leisure and the same financial resources. It is no criticism of a social utopia to say that the opportunities available to its inhabitants are not available to all the inhabitants of contemporary society. If they were, nobody would bother to try to realize the relevant utopia.

I do not see anything wrong with addressing an elite audience of »self-obsessed left intellectuals« (although I doubt that the average left intellectual is any more self-obsessed than the average construction worker). Changing the views of an intellectual elite is a traditional, and often effective, way to begin changing the self-descriptions of the citizenry as a whole. Nor do I see a problem about reconciling the need for strong poets (who really *are* more self-obsessed than most people) with the dialogical character of the self. The more strong poets, the more horizons there are to fuse. The more horizons get fused, the richer the possibilities opened by dialogue become. If we ever ran out of strong poets, culture and society would freeze over.

The construction workers of today can juggle ideas and develop aspirations that the construction workers of 500 B. C. could not. This is because, in the interim, a lot of strong poets came up with a lot of utopian visions, and made those visions attractive to intellectual elites. Eventually those visions trickled down to the masses. Dialogical rationality was one of the ideas that came along only after 500 B. C. We owe this idea primarily to Socrates – a strong poet who spent most of his time trying to convince an elite audience.

RESPONSE TO »THE LIBERAL IRONIST BETWEEN NATIONAL PRIDE AND GLOBAL SOLIDARITY«

Much of the argument of »The liberal ironist ...« seems to depend on the claim that allegiance to a nation-state is »a form of solidarity that is becoming politically obsolete«. I can easily agree that there is nothing sacred about the nation-state, just as there is nothing sacred about, say, fossil fuels. I hope both that the nation-state will eventually wither away and that we can eventually seal the coal mines and cap the oil wells. But until we can develop a hydrogen fusion reactor, or something similar, we have to do our planning for the human future on the assumption that fossil fuels will continue to be required. (They will be needed, for example, to melt the ores that make the metals that go into the computers on which we design fusion reactors. We work with what we have got.)

I think that we should acknowledge that only initiatives on the part of nation-states (either individually or through their representation in international organizations) can make it feasible for the farmers of Denmark to interact and cooperate with the peasants of Cambodia, or the construction workers of Benin with those of Paraguay. Only such initiatives are likely to make possible the development of what the authors call »extensive solidarity«. If nation-states had not signed the Universal Declaration of Human Rights, it would be much harder for human rights activists to accomplish anything. If nation-states had not signed on to the EU, the internationalism now being encouraged among Europeans would have been harder to endorse. Just as finding a way to replace fossil fuels requires burning up a lot of coal and petroleum, making the nation-state obsolete will require sustained efforts on the part of nation-states.

I do not think that anything I have written can be cited in support of the claim that I think of the nation-state as »a political equivalent of the self-contained subject« or »the only remaining guarantor for integrity and wholeness« or »the only remaining divinity«. I do not think that the process of extending »we-groups« as far as possible »soon finds its limits«. I am all in favor of extensive solidarity, and I of course agree with the authors that international solidarity among workers (or mothers, or birdwatchers, or philosophy professors) can come into existence without intervention on the part of nation-states.

I do not agree, however, that »I am a worker« and »I am an American« differ because the former, but not the latter, »refers to a significant quality that is actually *felt* to be shared«. There is nothing more natural or authentic about sharing the one identity than about sharing the other. Substituting extensive solidarity for national solidarity is not a matter of substituting an intrinsically better, or somehow deeper, sort of solidarity for an intrinsically worse, or somehow shallower, one. The sixteenth- and seventeenth century arguments for establishing and creating nation-states, and a sense of national citizenship, were pragmatic. So is the contemporary argument for creating extensive solidarity: Achieving it would help bring about, for example, nuclear disarmament, a global minimum standard of living, and many other good things.

The authors' favored scenario for political change seems to be one in which extensive solidarity among citizens of many countries becomes so powerful that it simply brushes national governments aside. This is an appealing bottom-up scenario, but I cannot imagine it being realized. For all the import-

ant moves toward internationalism in the course of the last sixty years have
been top-down initiatives. In both Europe and North America, the elites have
been dragooning the masses into adopting a cosmopolitan outlook – insisting
that national security can only be achieved by multilateral international agree-
ments, that more and more power has to be turned over to supra-national au-
thorities, and so on.

My hunch is that if the sort of extensive solidarity that the authors have
in mind is ever achieved, it will be because educated elites, through their control of the media, finally managed to instill loyalty to international institutions
in the citizenry, not because the citizens of each nation spontaneously reached
out to those of other nations.

Response to »Pragmatism, Realism, and Science«

It is hard to know how to argue about whether the work of Popper, Lakatos,
Kuhn, van Fraassen and Boyd has been, as the authors say it has, of »enormous practical significance«, or about whether it has »introduced new ideas of
great interest for scientists«. I agree with the authors that this is an empirical
question – one that has to be referred to historians and sociologists of
science. They may be in a position to find out how many scientists have
known, or cared, about the differences between the views of these various
philosophers. My own impression is that scientists are pretty unanimous in
their dislike for Kuhn, but not very familiar with his work nor with the debates to which it has given rise. The authors, however, have a different impression.

Another empirical question about which the authors and I disagree is
whether »adopting a pragmatic understanding of science« would deprive the
scientist of the »motivational and inspirational force which enables him to develop new ideas and methods«. This claim seems to me as implausible as the
suggestion that giving up a belief in God would deprive them of the conviction that they live in an orderly and intelligible universe. The authors may con-
ceivably be right in their prediction that a pragmatist culture would destroy
the scientists' morale. But I cannot imagine a research project (in sociology or
psychology) that would help us evaluate that prediction. We will probably not

find out until we are willing to perform a risky experiment in cultural change – one as risky as was the secularization of academic institutions.

It is also difficult to know whether the respect accorded to scientists in our society is due to their ability to provide us with such things as antibiotics and atomic bombs or, as the authors suggest, due to scientists being viewed as »discoverers of mind-independent features of an objective world, i. e., realists«. I rather doubt that the laity – that is, people outside of philosophy departments – are very clear about what »mind-independent« means. The authors take this notion as sufficiently clear as to be usable without further explanation, but of course a great deal of ink has been spilled over the question of what sense of »independence« is being used.

Their use of »mind-independent« is such that they interpret my claim that our causal relations with the world are the same when described in physicalist as in mentalistic terms as presenting me with a dilemma: either »the causal structure of the world is independent of us, hence a feature of the world in itself« or »causal relations are somehow imposed on the world by us«. My claim is that the choice between these two alternatives is one that we need not bother to make, since nothing can possibly turn on which alternative is chosen. Nobody would do anything different if they took one view rather than the other.

But the authors view this profession of indifference as »the plain confession of the lack of any argument«. It seems to me that they are saying: If you will not argue in our terms, we do not view you as arguing at all. But surely at many points in the history of philosophy, science, and politics, there have been occasions on which progress has been made by abandoning the terms in which an apparently irresolvable debate was being conducted. Can it really be the case that every time people have said »the old disputes were getting us nowhere; let us make a fresh start« their strategy constituted what the authors call »an unfair withdrawal from argument in favor of a propagandist strategy«?

If not arguing in the authors' terms means that I am making propaganda, so be it. I am propagandizing, practicing cultural politics. I am saying: let us try dropping some old terminology and see if we are any worse off. That is not an argument, it is a suggestion about an experiment which it profit us to perform. Is making such a suggestion *unfair*? It may be unwise – and if the authors are right in their empirical claims about the consequences of making this change, it is at least imprudent. But why unfair?

Another issue that divides me from the authors is that they have more use for notions such as »methods« and »standards of rationality« than I do. I have argued along Feyerabendian lines that there is nothing especially »scientific« about abductive reasoning. I think »abduction« names something that everybody does all the time. I have argued that what enables scientists to solve problems is what Kuhn called »initiation into a disciplinary matrix«, rather than the application of »standards of rationality«. This claim chimes with my view that forgetting about the realism-vs.-antirealism issue would leave »scientific practice, including experimental methods and the testing of hypotheses« unchanged. Yet the authors seem to think that I am under an obligation to show that such forgetfulness would result in scientists doing things differently.

Let me conclude these comments by discussing some paragraphs that I I found very puzzling. The authors say that I am unable to grant that »we all in fact do use the same general standards« when evaluating the rationality of somebody's behavior, and so am unable to agree with Davidson that rationality is a matter of »having a set of beliefs largely consistent and true«. But I take Davidson's point about the scheme-content distinction to be that we have no more use for the notion of incommensurable notions of rationality than we do for that of incommensurable conceptual schemes.

Neither Davidson nor I know what it would be to have a different »standard of rationality« than ours. I do not see what it is in my view that entails recognition of »the possibility that other standards of rationality exist and are in use, which are consistent in their own way of conceiving consistency.« Would not admitting that possibility mean admitting the possibility of a language untranslatable into our own? I cannot see what sort of wedge the authors hope to drive between me and Davidson. Certainly neither of us have any use for the notion of »a logic which deviates significantly from our logic«.

I am sorry if I gave the impression, in my writings or in discussion, that I think that »what truth, moral standards, logical laws and the like are depends on the conventions which a respective group of people has agreed on.« I have no use for the notion of »convention«. It is one thing to say, as I do, that the only test we have for truth or rightness or validity is coherence with our own beliefs. It is another to say that some other people's behavior might be so different than ours that we could find them intelligible but uncriticizable, thanks to their »different standard of rationality«. That is precisely the possibility that Davidson's argument for the necessity of charity excludes.

RESPONSE TO »IS RORTY'S NON-REDUCTIVE PHYSICALISM REDUCTIVE?«

I agree with Karakuş and Vieth that the term »epistemological behaviorism« is vague and misleading, and I now regret that I ever used either it or the term »physicalism« as a name for a position that I wished to hold. In my more recent writings, I have been urging that there is no need to have any view about what »really« exists – no need to have on ontology, and thus no need to distinguish between good metaphysics and bad metaphysics. All metaphysics is bad. So I have stopped calling myself a »naturalist«.

Even in those writings, however, I have sometimes used the term »naturalistic« as a term of praise for, among other things, Brandom's narrative about the coming into existence of the social norms that make possible the use of such linguistic items as singular terms and logical connectives. (Brandom himself, however, has no use for the term »naturalism«, which he thinks of as the attempt to somehow reduce the normative to the non-normative.) What I meant by calling that narrative »naturalistic« was merely that it gave us an account of intentionality that resembles Sellars' and differs from that of Chisholm and Searle. For Brandom and Sellars, there is no mystery about how intentionality came into the universe, because there is no mystery about how social norms did. For Chisholm and Searle, there is a mystery, because they regard intentionality as explaining our ability to erect social norms, rather than treating the latter as explaining the former.

I now think that »naturalistic« is too overworked and confusing a term to be serviceable. So instead of taking sides between strong and weak naturalism, I would prefer just to drop the topic. The authors' description of »weak« naturalism makes use of other notions (»immediacy«, »experience«) that I also have no use for. So, although I agree with the spirit of their criticisms of

strong naturalism, I do not wish to advocate weak naturalism either. I think
we would do better to abandon Dewey's attempt to construct a metaphysics
suitable for pragmatists, and instead interpret pragmatism as, among other
things, the claim that we do not need to have any views about what is real and
what is not (except in such particular contexts as »not real cream, but non-
dairy creamer« or »not a real diamond – just paste«).

Unlike Vieth and Karakuş, I do not think it helps to say that there are
»two realities with respect to methodology but only one with respect to ontology«. This is because I do not think that there is a tension between the manifest and the scientific image, or between the observer and the participant
point of view, that needs to be resolved by proclaiming an ontological
monism. It seems to me enough to say that we have many vocabularies at our
disposal, that we deploy each of them for somewhat different purposes, and
that all we need do is keep them out of each other's way. I do not see that
»the plurality of language games and the sections of knowledge next to one
another involve severe contradictions in our self-image«, nor that that plurality produces »severe practical dilemmas«, nor that there any other tensions that
philosophers need to iron out.

This is of course not to deny the existence of tensions – only to denigra-
te the importance of specifically philosophical ones. By contrast, there are (or
were) important tensions between Aristotelian and Newtonian discourses,
and between Catholic and Protestant language-games. But neither these nor
any of the other tensions between particular human projects can be resolved
by developing a better ontology or a better epistemology. If we give up the
idea of philosophy as a presiding super-science, we shall be better able to admit that the important tensions have to be settled *ambulando*, by the usual mes-
sy methods of cultural politics, rather than by elevating them to the level of
abstraction on which philosophical debates have traditionally been conducted.

Perhaps the crucial point at which my view diverges from that of the authors is that they, like Dewey, take the notion of »immediate experience«
seriously. I join Wittgenstein, Sellars and Brandom in rejecting the notion of
non-linguistic awareness, so I do not think that there is experience unmedia-
ted by language. Since I accept Sellars' »myth of Jones« (in his »Empiricism
and the Philosophy of Mind«) I think of our access to our own »inner life« as

no less linguistically mediated that our access to the colors of physical objects. I would not speak of realities being »accessible« or »inaccessible« from one or another perspective, as the authors do, since I think that our only cognitive access to anything is a matter of learning how to talk about it.

Instead of saying, as the authors do, that the felt differences between our practices »constitute the realm of being«, I would say that these felt differences constitute human life. Human beings continually invent new practices. Sellars' »Jones«, Luther, and Newton are examples of such inventiveness. As a result, human life becomes larger and richer. But there is no need to try to relate these practices to something outside all of them such as »immediate experience« or »basic reality«.

Response to »Skepticism, Correspondence, and Truth«

In a footnote, the authors say that externalism suffices to refute skepticism. I would prefer to say that externalism assumes the falsehood of skepticism. The authors are right that my argument against skepticism will appear circular to the skeptic, since my only reason for being an externalist is that externalists cannot be skeptics. Skepticism cannot be refuted once a representationist account of cognition is accepted. But an alternative account of cognition can be constructed that leaves no room for the skeptic to state his case. Leaving no such room counts, on my view, as an excellent reason for accepting that alternative. For no one would want to be a skeptic unless the only available account of the matter forced her to be.

I agree with the authors that all the skeptic needs is the theses they label (A) and (B). Conversely, all the anti-skeptic needs to do to make skepticism seem utterly implausible is to repudiate those two theses. But if one does repudiate them, one will not accept the authors' claim that »the content of my beliefs has to be accessible to me if they are to serve as reasons«, if that means »accessible to me without having to have knowledge of the causes of my beliefs and of the reactions of my interlocutors to my assertions«.

I accept Brandom's inferentialist account of content. He, like Davidson and Wittgenstein, starts from the premise that language and cognition are social phenomena, just as the internalist starts from the Cartesian premise that a person can mean something, and believe something, all by herself. What is accessible to me, on the Brandomian view, is the reactions of my fellow-speakers to my assertions, and the relations of those reactions to events in our common environment. This accessibility permits me to engage in what Davidson calls »triangulation«. My adjustment to those reactions causes me to continually change the content (that is, the inferential import) of the sentences I use to make assertions.

I agree that the game of giving and asking for reasons is »based on the idea that the content of our beliefs is at least fairly accessible to us«. But what we externalists mean by »content« is not what internalists mean. In our sense of the term, beliefs are not tertia. They are behavioral dispositions that are always in flux as a result of fresh encounters with one's surroundings. Since the content of a belief is its place in a network of inferences, Brandomians like myself must accept the counter-intuitive consequences that nobody has the same belief twice, that no two people share beliefs, and that a word never means the same thing twice.[1] These consequences follow from the fact that nobody ever draws quite the same inferences from an assertion as another person (or as himself at another moment), because their web of belief is constantly being rewoven.

I turn now from tertia to correspondence. The authors propose »correlation« as a replacement for »representation or isomorphism«. On their view, »how the correlation between sentences uttered in contexts and ways the world might be is a question psycho-linguists have to cope with«. But how are psycho-linguists supposed to cope with truths like »The square root of 2 is irrational« and »Love is better than hate«? How can the notion of »correlation« be applied once we move on to mathematics and morals? Why should perceptual reports serve as a model for all other true sentences?

The authors go on to say that the fact that some scientific theories are better tools than others shows that »the world is no longer indifferent to competing theories«. I can grant the point, if »indifferent« is used sufficiently loosely so as to permit us to say that the tree is not indifferent to competing axes, and that the tree arbitrates the competition between those axes. But when the terms are used in that way, the notion of »correspondence« is

1   These consequences are drawn, with satiric intent, by Fodor in the critique of Brandom which I cite in »The brain as hardware ...«.

trivialized. Certainly, as the authors say, »the world shows a kind of resistance«. But why identify the causal relation of resistance with the epistemic notion of arbitration? There is a difference between caused to change one's view
and having a rational arbitrator give one reasons for doing so.

The authors see a difference between being in a »metaphysical frame of
mind« and »struggling for a better fit of scientific predictions with reality«. I
think such attempts to give a sense to the notion of »fit« would be made only
by those attracted either by metaphysics or by skepticism. I see metaphysics
and skepticism as two sides of the same coin, one that I should like to take
out of circulation. Whereas the authors think of the philosophical tradition
that has given metaphysical or skeptical answers to the question »what is the
relation between mind or language and reality?« as having cultural value, I
think of that tradition as having exhausted whatever usefulness it might once
have had. It seems to me to have become a useless incumbrance. That is why
I welcome the Wittgenstein-Davidson-Brandom redescription of cognition
and of content. I suspect that my disagreement with the authors boils down
to our different evaluations of the cultural importance of an intellectual
tradition that I hope will wither away.

RESPONSE TO »STRONG AND WEAK METAPHYSICAL QUIETISM«

I am not sure that the atheism-agnosticism distinction is the right tool to use
in dissecting my views about truth. The trouble with the term »atheist« is that
it is applied indiscriminately to two different groups: those who think that
there fairly decisive evidence against God's existence (evidence such as the
existence of evil, for example, or the success of Darwinian accounts of the
origin of humanity) and those who simply have no views about God. The
latter typically cannot make much of the notion of »evidence for, or against,
the existence of God«. They do not know what would count as relevant evidence. So they would just like the word »God« to drop out of discourse. They
think that the presence of this term in the language may have done more
harm than good, and that we should try to get along without it – or, if we
must keep it, that we should give a sense that would make clear the debate
about whether God exists is pointless. (That was the sort of sense that the

theologian Paul Tillich tried to give »God«, in his book *Dynamics of Faith*, when he said that God is a symbol of the object of our ultimate concern.)

When it comes to truth, however, almost nobody argues either that there is, or that there is not, such a thing as truth. Philosophers do not debate the advisability of keeping the adjective »true« in the language. The question is usually not about the existence of an object, but about how much there is to say about the nature of the property signified by that adjective.

Some philosophers (Hilary Putnam, for example) have said that »true« is not the name of a property. I may have done so myself at some point: I would have to pore over my past writings before being sure whether I have or not. However that may be, I now find myself agreeing with Donald Davidson that one can cheerfully admit that »true« names a property of sentences while stoutly denying that the term can be given a definition, or even an interesting explication. On the view I now prefer, propertyhood is cheap, because *all* predicates name properties. »True« and »divine« each name a property, just as do »red«, »round and square« and »unicorn«. But in the case of »true« there is nothing interesting to say about the property named.

If there is a relevant analogue to »God«, it is not a nominalized adjective such as »truth« but rather »the Truth«, a definite description of the set of beliefs that correspond to the way the world really is – the set that is destined to be accepted at Peirce's »end of inquiry«. I do not believe that there is such a thing, I do not think that we can give a useful sense either to »really is« or to »corresponds«. So I would construe »being an atheist about truth« to mean »admitting that ›true‹ names a property, but wishing that the definite description »the Truth« might eventually drop out of discourse.

Heßbrüggen *et al.* suggest that I would do well to be agnostic, rather than atheistic, about »metaphysical beliefs«. But agnosticism here, as in the case of theological beliefs, is presumably the position that there may or not be such a thing as the Truth, or as the way the world really is – we just do not know. Putting the matter in those terms suggests that we do know what evidence would be relevant to the question. But I do not think that we have any clear sense of what such evidence would look like. Like the logical positivists, I think that when we realize that we have no idea what evidence bears on the existence of X, we should cease to use the term ›X‹ as the name of an object.

(Unlike the positivists, however, I do not think that »evidence« is always a matter of the deliverances of the senses. Any sort of evidence will do.)

The authors quote Putnam as asking me whether »If your aim is tolerance and the open society, would it not be better to argue for these directly, rather than to hope that these will come as the by-product of a change in our metaphysical beliefs?« I balk at the term »change in our metaphysical beliefs«. We do not say that somebody who has ceased to talk and think about God has changed his theological beliefs. Why should we attribute metaphysical beliefs to somebody who hopes that metaphysical issues will cease to be discussed?

So my answers to the two concluding questions posed by the authors are:

(1) The choice between atheism and agnosticism about »truth« is not a useful way to pose the issue, since it obscures the difference between the utility of an adjective and the utility of a definite description.

(2) I would prefer to find ways of avoiding metaphysics altogether, just as the positivists wanted to avoid theology altogether. »Metaphysics« in this sense includes adopting the attitude that we shall simply have to wait and see whether there is a way the world really is.

RESPONSE TO »THE WORLD REGAINED«

The big difference between Ludwig Siep's view and my own is that he would like to retain the idea of »the response of an independent reality« to human initiatives, as well as the notion of resistance to such initiatives. I see non-human things as resisting us, but not as responding to us – getting in our way, but not providing information about themselves to us. Whereas he wants »a mix of coherence and correspondence theories of truth« I can find as little use for the notion of »corresponding to reality« as I do for that of »reality responding«.

Siep and I share the same utopian vision of a planet in which there are »worldwide conventions about the preservation of diversity of species and landscapes, about sustainable development, cultural pluralism and the protection of human rights.« But he sees this utopia as having something to do with

the way the world is independently of our descriptions of it, and also as having something to do with »the human ›essence‹«. I can find no use for either
notion – no way of bringing either to bear in arguments over which utopian
vision to pursue.

I do not see, for example, how one would back up a claim that a world
without gender discrimination is more natural, or more faithful to our humanity, than one in which one gender is subservient to another. The latter
sort of world is the one in which all human beings except the most recent inhabitants of the the rich Western democracies have lived. I am very glad that
the feminists' utopian vision has recently triumphed in those countries, but I
would not know how to argue that gender equality is more faithful to something ahistorical than gender inequality.

Siep and I agree that »it is only on the basis of well-founded experiences
that we can ask for the right conditions ... and the good consequences of actions and norms for a world approvable without restrictions«. But I would
put no weight on the word »well-founded«, and would prefer to omit it. Siep
wishes to preserve the notion of well-foundedness, I take it, because he thinks
that our »shared value experiences« are »about something which can resist our
wishes and volitions, and can reverse our expectations and prejudices«. I do
not see how to get from »things resist our wishes« to »modifications in our
beliefs and decisions made as a result of such resistance are better founded
than those that do not«. As I see it, *all* such modifications are made as a result
of the resistance of things. Both the West's decision to give women the vote
and the Taliban's decision to expel women from universities were made as a
result of such resistance. For resistance, in this wide sense, is just a matter of
encountering untoward consequences.

I take it that Siep wishes to preserve the notions of resistance and correspondence because he thinks of the moral progress the West has made as
bringing it into better conformity with something that was already there –
something that has been resisting us, and has thereby forced us to act differently so as to encounter less resistance. But accepting or rejecting this metaphor of being shaped by things in order to conform better to them does
not, as far as I can see, make a difference to practice. Both the feminists and
the Taliban think of themselves as having made moral progress, and both are

in an equally good position to pride themselves on better conformity to Siep's
»good world«.

Perhaps this metaphor of conformity is harmless. It is certainly an improvement on »conformity to the will of God«, because it does not encourage
theocracy. But I would prefer to dispense with it in order to make room for
the idea that the utopian visions that inspire political action – both the good
ones and the bad ones – are free creations of the human imagination. I do not
see that the notion of »a structured and ordered world« – cosmos as opposed
to chaos – adds anything to the notion of »a better world«. I agree with Siep
that a world in which human beings have obligations to non-human species
would be a better world than one in which they do not, but I do not see that
our preference for such a world requires us to »regain« a world. Once we give
up on what Siep calls »an absolute reality behind all ... theories and evaluations«, I do not think that enough remains of the notion of »a structured and
ordered world« to make it worth preserving.